A Stroll Through

MODERNISTA BARCELONA

© 1999 Ediciones Polígrafa, S. A.
Balmes, 54 - 08007 Barcelona (Spain)

© Original Spanish text: Lluís Permanyer
© Photographs: Melba Levick,
except p. 22 at bottom: Jordi Pareto (Turisme de Barcelona);
p. 99 at bottom: Pere Vivas and pp. 158 and 159: Martí Gasull
Disigned by Estudi Carme Vives
Translated by Richard Rees

I.S.B.N.: 84-343-0879-7
D.L.: B. 6.322-1999 (Printed in Spain)

Colour separations by Alfacrom, Barcelona

A Stroll Through MODERNISTA BARCELONA

Text: Lluís Permanyer

Photographs: Melba Levick

INSTITUT MUNICIPAL DEL
PAISATGE URBÀ
I LA QUALITAT DE VIDA

Ajuntament de Barcelona

Ediciones Polígrafa

Contents

Foreword

In contrast to other cities of the world, Barcelona is not characterized by any one edifice in particular, but rather by the *Eixample*, a nineteenth-century city expansion that is replete with the bold, sinuous buildings of *Modernisme*. It is here that Antoni Gaudí, Josep Puig i Cadafalch, and Lluís Domènech i Montaner, among other architects, left the stamp of their creativity and set a style that has made the Barcelonans a people who truly appreciate architecture.

This book presents a large part of our art nouveau (or *modernista*, as it was called here) heritage and draws us deeply into a movement that went beyond the merely cultural sphere to become a way of life. It immerses us in dynamic turn-of-the-century Barcelona, the creative city that chose to open itself to Europe rather than to lament the loss of Spain's last colonies, and displayed its exuberance in the works of such artists as Isaac Albéniz, Ramon Casas, Pablo Picasso, Darío de Regoyos, Santiago Rusiñol, and Miquel Utrillo.

Barcelona has preserved this heritage and strives to make it better known. Initiatives such as the Art Nouveau Route reflect this determination. In short, this book is an indispensable tool for anyone who, in addition to appreciating the architectural gems of Barcelona's art nouveau period, wishes to understand a movement that embodied as no other the innovating spirit of our city.

Joan Clos
Mayor of Barcelona

Barcelona Is Modernisme

Modernisme was Barcelona's Renaissance in both senses of the term: as a formal style and as a societal rebirth. There are two moments in the history of the twenty centuries of Barcelona that clearly and spectacularly mark the city we admire today: the Gothic and its counterpart at the other end of imperial Spain's rapid rise and long decline, *Modernisme*. It need not surprise us that *Modernisme* reached such heights of spectacle, since it was as the manifestation of a positive, creative, and dynamic social explosion. The recent centennial of the disastrous Spanish-American War of 1898 sharply highlighted the different attitudes that reigned in Spain on the one hand, and in Barcelona on the other, immediately following the loss of Spain's last colonies a hundred years ago. Indeed, the despair, crisis, and depression of Spain at large contrasted with the euphoria and rising prosperity of Barcelona. While the rest of Spain became disconcerted and forlornly inward-looking, Barcelona turned its gaze toward Europe, where it found inspiration.

It was in Europe that Barcelona discovered *Modernisme*, a style that in each country blossomed under a different name: "art nouveau" in Great Britain; "modern style" in France (in English, to reflect the style's English roots); "Jugendstil" in Germany; "Sezessionstil" in Austria; "art 1900" in Belgium; "stile Liberty" in Italy (after the London store promoted the style). And in Barcelona it was called *Modernisme*, a term that reflected its embrace of the new century and its rejection of the past. But wherever the movement took hold, it brought with it innovations and implied a way of seeing and reflecting on the past and the present that deviated from orthodoxies of all types, and particularly, the Catholic countries, from the line dictated by the Vatican. Indeed, the pope saw new ideas as so radical that he went so far as to condemn them as dangerous. But in Barcelona, the movement could not be limited to a new style in the decorative arts. Modernity was its essence; the adoption of the name *Modernisme* left no doubt as to the nature of the Catalan ambitions.

It was nothing new that Barcelona should admire Europe, since far from adopting a stance of introversion and isolation, throughout her history the city had invariably looked beyond her frontiers. Her geographical position—on the Mediterranean and near the border with the rest of Europe—and lack of natural resources led to the need for commerce and the readiness to make deals and be a cosmopolitan. Thus it is understandable that *Modernisme* should have been cultivated only in Barcelona and in those areas where Barcelona exercised influence: Catalonia, Valencia and the Balearic Islands. And even in Melilla: it was in this North African city that the architect Nieto, highly influenced by Antoni Gaudí, did his military service, subsequently remaining there and introducing *modernista* architecture, cultivated also by other professionals and today considered a proud sign of local identity.

Modernisme represented the crystallization of many trends in Catalan society at the end of the nineteenth century. The decadence that had firmly set in over many centuries was finally dying and political nationalism was beginning to bear fruit. The Catalan economy was enjoying a period of exceptional prosperity, and large amounts of capital from abroad and from the rural areas sought refuge in Barcelona. As the biggest and best planned urban expansion in Europe (the Eixample) was being developed, the city was beginning to recover a spirit of confidence in her immediate future. The elite were convinced that they would soon be the protagonists of a historic moment. All these elements converged at the same time and in the same direction, and the major, original, and creative architectural style that came to predominate was a further reflection of this crucial moment. It would have been unthinkable at the time to continue with something as neutral, insipid, and banal as the architectural eclecticism that had been the style for much of the nineteenth century, fruit of its period of recession, with nothing better to do than turn its gaze toward the past in order to recover its familiar symbols: columns, pediments, moldings, and so on.

The signs of the movement went far beyond characteristic styles—of architecture, sculpture, painting, poetry, theater, and the decorative arts—to be evident in the artists themselves. However, the movement went far beyond this, was much deeper and wider in scope. The *modernista* creator was immediately recognizable as such, since he let his hair and beard grow long, dressed in black, and invariably wore a wide-brimmed hat. He would smoke tobacco and other more potent drugs that would transport him to artificial paradises. He was an impassioned bohemian, enamored of everything new. There was therefore a *modernista* way of understanding and experiencing life.

At the close of the 1888 Barcelona Universal Exposition, a number of key *modernistas* met at the exposition's Café-Restaurant; designed by Lluís Domènech i Montaner, to reflect on the main principles that were to inform the style that was emerging with such suggestive force. Such was the spirit of that coterie that they engaged in long discussions not only on architecture and craftsmanship but also on politics and nationalism. "What forms or sources of inspiration are we to cultivate?" these committed men eagerly asked themselves. They were aware that destiny had provided them with the opportunity to if not construct, at least to reconstruct the city and their homeland and provide them with an image to show the world. They were convinced that they were the protagonists and creators of a historical moment. Such politicization induced them to turn their gaze to the past, beyond the centuries of decline to the era when Barcelona and Catalonia were a power or even *the* imperial Mediterranean power, which at that time meant the world, since the course of Western history unfolded around that sea of civilization. Hence the Romanesque and themes that pervade Gothic *Modernisme*. The rediscovery of the Romanesque period in fact, was due in part to the work of the architect, historian, and politician Josep Puig i Cadafalch, who was the driving force (together with the critic Josep Pijoan) behind the salvation of a key Romanesque artifact, the Pyrenean murals.

In realizing the ambitions of *Modernisme*, Barcelona had two unique resources. First was the city's still-intact community of craftsmen. *Modernisme's* inexhaustible variety stems in part from the movement's close links to this community: all the movement's architects turned to the imagination of magnificent artisans who skillfully enriched their works by interpreting the ideas expressed in sketches, both finished and unfinished. In Barcelona the artisan tradition dated from medieval times and had been preserved ever faithful to the highest levels of quality. Some scholars have proposed that the host of professional craft workshops in existence in Barcelona around the turn of the century was possible thanks to the spectacle and richness of *Modernisme*, and not vice-versa. But such a tradition would have been impossible to improvise. What was possible, on the other hand, was to send a number of artisans abroad to perfect their craft or extend their knowledge. One such craftsman was the mosaicist, Lluís Bru, who, following the advice of Domènech i Montaner, went to Italy in order to learn the techniques of Roman mosaics. Without craftsmen capable of delicate handwork, it is questionable whether *Modernisme's* characteristic aesthetic of restless movement could have been realized. Unlike the more controlled movement of the baroque, *Modernisme's* movement is highlighted everywhere with the *fuetada* (*coup de fouet* or whiplash), that interminable stem-and-flower motif that meanders through and fills *modernista* spaces; it also appears in less descriptive form, such as in the triumph art curves of La Pedrera, the sinuous stone that dominates the whole facade.

Barcelona's other great asset was its spectacular new building site the *Eixample*, the plans for which had been drawn up and executed just under two decades before by the engineer Ildefons Cerdà. The *Eixample* not only provided sufficient room to accommodate everyone's tastes, its identical streets afforded architects with an unprecedented opportunity to show off their facades. Accustomed as the people of Barcelona were to the narrowness and congestion of a city straitjacketed by her walls, as soon as the *Eixample* began to be developed all doubts were dispelled about whether this meant a definite improvement. As evidence of this one need only contemplate the virtuosity of Casa Batlló and the Palau Güell: it was clear that Cerdà's gridiron layout provided an incomparable added value. It has often been said that architectural excesses of *modernista* facades must be interpreted as the will to offset with eccentricity the uniformity imposed by the Cerdà plan. I do not subscribe to this view. *Modernista* architects would have designed their buildings in exactly the same way, regardless of the site where they would eventually stand; proof of this is the fact that elsewhere in Barcelona they executed projects with the same dazzlingly differential fervor.

Barcelonans with sufficient capital at their disposal to erect a new building, believed from the very outset in the thrilling adventure of the *Eixample*. They did not hesitate to abandon the rural family seats they had inherited and choose an architect of renown to design their new residence, whether single- or multi-family. In the latter case they would occupy the first floor, which thus came to be known as the *planta principal* (main floor). Thus healthy social competition began to ascertain which were the best of the newly erected buildings in the setting of the *Eixample*. Everyone rushed to participate, and architects contributed the best, most audacious designs of which they were capable. There is no other period in the whole of the history of the city to compare with this one. The freedom and scope for eccentricity that *Modernisme* provided was decisive here. It was not very long before Barcelona became a city distinguished by self-perpetuating variety, unlike other capitals and cities dominated by uniformity offset here and there by the occasional palace. Indeed, since the city lacked a royal family and was not a national capital, palaces, in the strict sense of the word, don't really exist in Barcelona, though some extremely sumptuous, though relatively small, houses were built by the bourgeoisie and the aristocracy.

Such dazzling disorder was not understood at the time, above all by foreigners. Georges Clemenceau for one. In 1910, having lost the presidency of the French government, Clemenceau was nearing the end of a long lecture tour in Latin America. He returned to Europe by sea and docked in Barcelona. The trustees of the Barcelona Athenaeum went to visit him at the Hotel Colón, in Plaça de Catalunya, and invited him to give a lecture the following day. Clemenceau gladly accepted. Later that day he took a carriage up Passeig de Gràcia, whose architectural fantasies so displeased him that when he reached La Pedrera he was so outraged that he ordered the coachman to return immediately to the hotel. He refused to give his lecture in a city of such hare-brained diversity and returned to Paris, whereupon reporters bombarded him with questions. He hastened to make it clear that he had fled not from his tour of Latin America but from a Barcelona so absurd that they were even building houses for dragons. In 1929 the novelist Evelyn Waugh, for his part, declared on contemplating Casa Batlló that it must be the Turkish consulate, since no one could imagine any other purpose behind such a bizarre facade.

Harder to understand than attacks by foreigners is why, in 1920, a campaign of discredit was launched within Barcelona itself to undermine the prestige that *Modernisme* had won for the city. What began as an intellectual movement—really a reaction against everything associated with modernism—called *Noucentisme*, became, by the 1930s, a call to action, with some examples of *modernista* architecture falling victim to the irreparable action of the pickax. Intellectuals, historians, and art critics ruthlessly attacked *modernista* works until such a negative atmosphere had been created that the mutilations and demolitions were looked upon with enthusiastic approval. The writer Josep Pla, among others, proposed in the 1940s that all the ornamentation of the Palau de la Música Catalana be removed. The Palau Güell was on the point of being sold to be dismantled and rebuilt stone by stone on the other side of the Atlantic. Casa Fuster, at the upper end of Passeig de Gràcia, was on the point of being demolished by none other than its owners, the ENHER electrical company. The facade and above all the *planta principal* of Casa Lleó Morera suffered from irreparable amputations. The luster of a great number of *modernista* buildings was dimmed by the addition of a number of stories of alarming, shameful mediocrity. The Barcelona city council did nothing to protect that heritage, disconcerted as they were by criticisms that discredited and disparaged *Modernisme*. Why was this campaign launched? Perhaps the novelist Gustave Flaubert had the answer when he wrote "le mauvais gout est le gout de la génération antérieure". For the fact is that the *noucentistes* hated everything the previous generation had left them so much that all they desired was to destroy them.

The first to come to the rescue of *Modernisme* were Salvador Dalí and the surrealists in the mid-1930s. The great painter eulogized, to bizarre extremes, the works of what he termed "edible architecture." What really saved them from destruction, however, was the discovery in the United States of the oeuvre of Antoni Gaudí, thanks to the major New York exhibition organized by George R. Collins in 1952.

Once *Modernisme's* former glory had been restored in people's minds, the next step was to make the buildings themselves dazzling again. Thanks to the memorable restoration campaign launched in connection with the 1992 Barcelona Olympics under the slogan "Barcelona posa't guapa" (Barcelona, make yourself beautiful), the world discovered that the city was not gray but merely dirty. Indeed the results of the campaign were so unexpected, spectacular, and enthralling that polychrome facades were reborn that even the Barcelonans themselves never imagined were there. The challenge of hosting the Olympic Games had led to the rediscovery of all the quality, grandeur, and color of *Modernisme*, so that today Barcelona is again synonymous with *Modernisme*, the best *Modernisme*.

① Palau Güell
1886–1890
Carrer Nou de la Rambla 3–5

Antoni Gaudí i Cornet, *architect*

The relationship between Antoni Gaudí and industrialist Eusebi Güell began almost as love at first sight. In Paris, Güell was so impressed by a certain display case for gloves that he saw that he did not rest until he had met the designer. When the occasion took place, Güell realized at once that this was the man for whom he was looking—an architect who would distinguish him from the rest of the Barcelona bourgeoisie. Güell commissioned Gaudí to design the pavilions for his vast estate, on the site of what would later be the Avinguda Diagonal. Their working relationship was perfect, and for this reason Güell entrusted the architect with a far more important commission, one for which Gaudí would be granted total liberty to follow the dictates of his brilliant imagination. The work in question was Güell's own residence.

The choice of site was an unusual one at a time when the aristocracy and the haute bourgeoisie had decided from the very outset to embark on the adventure of the Eixample. Güell had inherited the site, which stood next to the family residence occupying numbers 35 and 37 on the nearby Rambla. He asked the architect to build a palace that would complement and enrich the house and be linked to it by

means of a gallery, which would cross the inner courtyard. This part of the palace was conceived as a public area for parties, meetings, receptions, and even concerts. Another section of the palace would provide accommodation for guests.

Knowing that he had been granted absolutely free rein, Gaudí put together a team of highly reputed artisans and artists, all determined to give their best: the painter Aleix Clapés; the sculptor Joan Flotats; the decorator Antoni Oliva; the architect Camil Oliveras (who in this case acted as decorator); the blacksmiths Joan Oños, Salvador Gabarrós, and the Badia brothers; the carpenter Julià Soley; the joiner Eudald Puntí; and the Ventura brothers, monumental masons.

The main facade, by virtue of the quality of the materials used and its air of solemnity, already reveals that this is no ordinary house. A passerby realized this on the first day the facade was revealed, and made a highly disparaging comment, unaware that Gaudí and Güell, who were contemplating the recently completed work, were listening. "In that case, I like it even more!" exclaimed Güell. He was delighted by this negative reaction, since it was exactly what he was hoping for: to distinguish himself from the common herd of the haute bourgeoisie thanks to the genius of the architect.

Possibly the most important element on this slightly asymmetrical facade is the wrought-iron coat of arms. On the other hand, the rear facade is far more audacious and innovative, especially in the daring form of the gallery.

The interior holds three main spaces, each of which harbors a wealth of astonishing details.

There are three main spaces.

First, the hall and the descent to the coach house by means of a helicoidal ramp. The visitor would never expect that such a secondary element could be so beautiful and original. The thickness of the columns and the quality Gaudí managed to extract from the humblest of materials create a fascinating and highly unusual whole.

Second, the main salon on the first floor. A visitor here must take the time to examine both the whole and the details, for Gaudí's genius can be appreciated even in the apparently most insignificant elements. What is most worthy of attention here is the verticality of the ascending void, which endows the space with a grandeur difficult to describe.

Third, the flat roof or *terrat*, highly typical of Mediterranean cities. Gaudí transformed the chimneys and ventilators into a forest of sculpture presided over by the needlelike dome over the main salon. The

richness of forms imaginatively clad in the ceramic fragments known as *trencadís* heralds what the architect would later accomplish on a larger, more spectacular scale in La Pedrera. Some of these structures, which were not completed in Gaudí's day, were embellished in 1994 by several artists and architects.

Shortly after the Spanish Civil War this gem was about to be lost because an American millionaire was negotiating not only its purchase but, worse still, its stone-by-stone transfer to the other side of the Atlantic. Fortunately, the building was acquired by the Barcelona city council, who not only salvaged it but carried out an exemplary restoration operation, directed by the architect Antonio González Moreno-Navarro.

② THE GAUDÍ LAMPPOSTS
1879
Plaça Reial

ANTONI GAUDÍ I CORNET, *architect*

Barcelona's Plaça Reial, designed in 1848 by Francesc Molina i Casamajó, features two lampposts that Gaudí created in his youth. He had worked for the master builder Josep Fontserè, who had executed major projects for the City Hall, and it is for this reason that in 1879 he was entrusted with the project for street lighting, which at that time consisted of gas lamps.

Gaudí's project, though considerably idiosyncratic, does not yet fully reveal his genius. Although the work is not strictly *modernista*, given the architect's subsequent career it cannot be overlooked. This model consists of six branches; another pair of three-branched lampposts was placed in 1889 before the side entrance to the civil governor's headquarters, overlooking the Pla del Palau. An elegant combination of wrought iron and bronze, subtly ornamented, the lamppost stands on a solid stone base. The crowning element is Gaudí's personal version of Mercury's helmet, which he had conceived when together with Fontserè he designed the railings that surround the Parc de la Ciutadella.

The recent restoration is correct except for the colors of the Barcelona coat of arms, which do not correspond to those of the original project.

③ Hotel España

1904
Carrer de Sant Pau 9–11

Lluís Domènech i Montaner, *architect*

The Fonda España, created by Joan and Pau Riba, opened its doors in the 1850s. The business soon prospered, which led the brothers to extend and modernize it. The converted establishment was renamed the Grand Hotel d'Espagne, as commemorated by an acid-etched glass pane. Domènech i Montaner was entrusted with the project. When the project was completed in 1904, the city awarded it the diploma that can now be seen framed in the main salon.

The elegant foyer features columns, brass lamps, and sgraffiti.

The bar was subsequently mutilated, although the impressive fireplace, carved in alabaster by Alfons Juyol, has been preserved. The sculptural group, by Eusebi Arnau, evokes the passing of time in the human body, from birth to old age, and the whole ensemble is presided over by the coat of arms of Spain.

The inner patio features feminine figures in the style of Alphonse Mucha, who wish guests good morning and good night; the staircase is decorated with sgraffiti and mosaics.

The most important elements, however, are the two dining rooms. The one at the far end is characterized by a huge mural, maritime in theme and featuring mermaids, which some have attributed to the painter Ramon Casas, although there is no objective evidence to support this view. Whoever the artist was, he was certainly a great professional, as we see from the way he drew the faces and, above all, the waves, which serve as ornamental borders. The banisters are masterworks of joinery enriched with glazed ceramic, decorated with the coats of arms of different cities and kingdoms of Spain. All is illuminated by the outstanding brass lamps.

Although the other dining room may seem less spectacular at first sight, on the whole it is richer and better finished, its joinery work almost sculptural in quality. The stained-glass windows, the mosaics, and the brass lamps are all fine examples of craftsmanship.

It is a great shame that despite much research on the subject, it has proven impossible to ascertain the names of the artisans who worked under Domènech i Montaner's inspired guidance. On the other hand, we are fortunate to have received this legacy at all; its preservation seems almost miraculous, given the neglect it suffered. Indeed, for several decades the first-mentioned dining room was a warehouse. On the other hand, perhaps it is precisely because of this neglect that it has been preserved, since nobody was tempted to bother with modernizing it.

4 Farmàcia del doctor Genové

1911
Rambla, 77

Enric Sagnier i Villavecchia, *architect*

Despite the fact that the site owned by Doctor Genové was far from inspiring, since it was very narrow, in this project the architect Enric Sagnier i Villavecchia revealed an indisputable professionalism. The only surviving facade from the original project has a somewhat neo-Gothic air. On the ground floor, where the pharmacist's shop was, he built an impressive pointed arch, the key of which is enriched by a relief evoking Asclepius, the god of medicine. The floors above were originally occupied by a laboratory. Arches and eaves elegantly crown the building. A major element is the refined work by the renowned mosaic artist Lluís Bru (who also did the mosaics for the Palau de la Música Catalana and Casa Lleó Morera), in blue and gilt, heightened by calligraphy denoting the function of the building. This calligraphy has unfortunately disappeared due to the frequent changes of ownership (the building has been a shoeshop, a bazaar, and now houses the head office of Promoció de Ciutat Vella). Also lost are the wrought-iron banner and the stained-glass windows advertising the establishment.

Inside, period advertisements evoke a certain nostalgic air: "Dr. Genové's salicylic water. Tonic, balsam, disinfectant, pleasant odor" or "The best skin cream, Genové's (salicylic) cream."

⑤ ANTIGA CASA FIGUERAS

1902
Rambla 83

ANTONI ROS I GÜELL, *painter and decorator*

The noodle maker Jaume Figueras first set up his business in Carrer de Sant Ramon, later moving to the Rambla on the corner of Carrer Petxina. As his business was thriving, in 1902 it occurred to him to carry out alterations to his establishment in accordance with the *modernista* style then in vogue. Directed by Antoni Ros, a landscape painter, stage designer, and decorator, he put together a team of renowned professionals: Lambert Escaler was responsible for the symbolist sculpture on the facade; Rigalt & Granell for the symbolist stained-glass windows; M. Vilà i Domènech for the metalwork; J. M. Bernadors for the interior ornamental sculpture; Mario Maragliano (author of the frieze on the stage of the Palau de la Música) for the mosaics; Boix for the painting; Corrius for the marble; Medemant for the carpentry; F. Lacambra for the copperwork; and the Badia brothers for the locksmithing.

Modernisme represented the triumph of the curve, and this establishment is privileged in that it stands on a sensually curving street corner. The facade is enriched by the presence of a fine peacock.

When the establishment was eventually closed everything seemed to suggest that it would be demolished. However, in 1986, thanks to the pastry chef Antoni Escribà, it was saved. Not only did Escribà buy the building, he also refurbished it so that his son Christian could continue the family pastry and bakery business.

⑥ CATALANA DE GAS I ELECTRICITAT

1895
Avinguda del Portal de l'Àngel 20–22

JOSEP DOMÈNECH I ESTAPÀ, *architect*

Josep Domènech i Estapà, known as "Domènech the Bad" as opposed to the author of the Palau de la Música Catalana (Lluís Domènech i Montaner), always remained somewhat aloof from *Modernisme* and even published theoretical writings against the movement. Even so, he could not entirely escape its influence. This work is possibly the most *modernista* of the whole of his output. The monumental quality of the facade reveals, even to someone totally unversed in the subject, that this is neither a private building nor a single-family residence. Symmetry, balance, and heaviness are the main characteristics, not to mention ornamental austerity. The top part is the most successful, although the whole, given the high quality of the materials used, exudes the air of distinction required by the client, at that time every bit a commercial leader of the city. It is the foyer, rather than the entrance, that displays the sumptuousness typical of these establishments. The side facade, at no. 3, Carrer de Montsió, is of a simplicity appropriate to an entrance strictly for employees.

(7) CASA FRANCESC MARTÍ I PUIG (ELS QUATRE GATS)
1896
Carrer de Montsió 3 bis

JOSEP PUIG I CADAFALCH, *architect*

The first project by Puig i Cadafalch, Casa Francesc Martí i Puig, is an apartment building, in which the owner lived on the first floor. At first sight, what strikes the observer is the color of one of the materials used: brick. This is the reason why the art historian Alexandre Cirici i Pellicer defines Puig i Cadafalch's *modernista* phase as his red period, as opposed to his subsequent white and pink periods. The other material is stone, used mostly in the door and window frames, except for the arches and galleries, and in the ornamental elements, which were sculpted by Eusebi Arnau, the architect's faithful collaborator from that moment onwards.

Puig i Cadafalch's particular brand of *Modernisme* was the result, as in the case of other colleagues of his, of a backward glance at the Gothic, the period that evoked Catalonia's glorious past, to which he added differentiating touches in the form of Dutch or German reminiscences, visible in this case in the form of the ground-floor pointed arches and the heraldic motifs.

A decorative element that appears on the corner and which would be present in all of Puig i Cadafalch's *modernista* buildings is the evocation of Sant Josep (Saint Joseph), which in his case is a manifestation of political *Catalanisme*, a further aspect of the architect's commitment. The vaulted niche is empty, since the image of Sant Jordi disappeared during riots. The entrance to the building was highlighted by a complex interpretation of the Martí i Puig family coat of arms, the whole ensemble sculpted by Arnau.

Also worthy of note is the fine wrought-iron work, executed by Manuel Ballarín and featured on the balconies and the railings that close Passatge del Patriarca, a private mews.

This building was to become famous for reasons other than purely architectural ones, for in 1897 the literary café Els Quatre Gats opened on the ground floor. Founded by Pere Romeu and Miquel Utrillo and funded by the banker Manuel Girona, it was a nest of young artists, such as Picasso, who exhibited there for the first time in 1900 and designed the menu. Although the establishment had an ephemeral existence, its fame has lasted much longer than its lifespan. Evidence of this is the fact that the interior, miraculously preserved (it was transformed into a warehouse), was restored just over a decade ago. Although the large painting of the tandem bicycle is a copy by Arranz Bravo and Bartolozzi of the original, which was acquired by the Museu d'Art Modern when the establishment closed, the interior still retains a certain period feel, enhanced by the photographs preserved from the time when bearded Romeu ruled with authority and maliciousness, hanging framed on the walls alongside drawings by Picasso.

(8) PALAU DE LA MÚSICA CATALANA
1908
Carrer de Sant Pere Més Alt 11 / Carrer de Amadeu Vives 1

LLUÍS DOMÈNECH I MONTANER, *architect*

The Orfeó Català was founded in 1891. So quickly did it acquire prestige that in 1904 it was decided to build a venue for the choir in keeping with its renown. Today we might wonder why such a cramped site was chosen, although the main reason for the choice was one of convenience: it came as close as possible to where most of the choir members and associates lived. The architect demonstrated his skill by taking as much advantage as possible of such a potentially unrewarding site. The inauguration ceremony took place in February 1908.

The facade is of bare red brick featuring mosaics by Lluís Bru (this fact was recorded in an inscription at the bottom of one of the openings in the entrance columns, that served as ticket offices), sculpted heads and two domes, one of which was damaged and will perhaps be reconstructed one day. However, the whole epic force of the ensemble is concentrated in the sculpture by the prestigious *modernista* artist Miquel Blay, the inspiration for which was the theme of the traditional song. This facade in a way disguises another facade, entirely of glass, which as a kind of pioneer curtain wall serves to bathe the concert hall in enriching natural light. Consequently, the best time to visit the Palau is when the interior is enhanced by the light provided by nature, and it is not surprising that the ornamentation that completely covers the interior is a kind of recreation of a greenhouse, a motif much cultivated by pictorial *Modernisme*.

Outstanding aspects of the concert hall are the great stained-glass dome by Rigalt & Granell; the sculpted stage mouth prosenium, designed by Domènech and executed by Dídac Masana and Pau Gargallo, which anticipated cubism by using assemblage (the spears and reins held by the Valkyries); the back of the stage with sculptures by Eusebi Arnau and mosaics by Mario Maragliano; and a whole series of mosaics by Bru scattered throughout the hall. All representations of the four stripes of the Catalan flag were concealed by government order during the Franco regime. It was decided to use curtains, an optimal solution since Franco insisted on their destruction.

The effect produced by this hall on the occasion of concerts is fascinating, and I have it on authority that the great musicians who have performed here have all confessed their thrill on doing so.

In the eighties it became clear that the institution had to be brought into line with the demands of the present day. To this end, Oscar Tusquets, Diaz & Associates were engaged. The spectacular result was obtained thanks to the team's deep understanding of and respect for Domènech i Montaner's art. The most important intervention was not the transformation of the whole prosaic, functional sector hidden behind the concert hall but the alterations to the side facade, increasing the penetration of natural light blocked by the neighboring parish church of Sant Francesc de Paola, part of which was reduced in size. (An agreement will soon be signed with the archbishopric which will allow the removal of the church and the extension of the Palau facade.) The whole of the ground floor was occupied by the offices of the Orfeó. Now the wooden partitions have been removed to give way to an impressive foyer, a fitting welcome to music lovers. More complex and delicate was the intervention in the concert hall. The removal of two boxes widened the stage, and the stalls were replaced by seating designed by Tusquets. The architect's master stroke, however, was the introduction of air conditioning without the need for intrusive installations. The feat consisted of opening small circular holes in each dark leaf covering the ceiling, the installation thus remaining discreetly hidden.

The two staircases that permit access to the gallery above constitute an ornamental transition between the differential styles that mark both spaces. The architect David Mackay has written that reaching the top of the staircase and discovering the hall is one of the greatest thrills modern architecture has given him.

Late in 1987 UNESCO declared the Palau de la Música Catalana, a World Heritage site, and rightly so, I believe. It is the most *modernista* building in the world.

⑨ CASA PONS / PASCUAL
1891
Passeig de Gràcia 2 and 4

ENRIC SAGNIER I VILLAVECCHIA, *architect*

The brothers Alexandre Maria and Isidra Pons i Serra reached an agreement with Sebastià Pascual to jointly carry out a single project that would undoubtedly give distinction to the large estate framed by a number of different streets, which would make it possible to create facades, unusual in an *Eixample* characterized by buildings between party walls. Sagnier, a competent professional, managed to

find the solemn, elegant language of a restrained *Modernisme* in neo-Gothic style. He coordinated a team consisting of the stonemason Francesc Pastor, the metalworkers Emili Farrés and Josep Lagarriga, the stained-glass window maker Antoni Rigalt, the carpenter Magí Vilardell and the joiner Josep Recasens. The external profile, restored in 1984, retains the original appearance; on the other hand, of the inner decor that enriched the two independent entrances and the owners' first floors practically nothing remains. From the street it is possible to contemplate the leaded stained-glass windows featuring medieval personalities. In 1905 there was a dairy on the ground floor designed by the painter Alexandre de Riquer.

⑩ Casa Calvet

1900
Carrer de Casp 48

Antoni Gaudí i Cornet, *architect*

In 1898 the widow of the textile industrialist Pere Màrtir i Carbonell commissioned Gaudí to build a house between party walls in the most exclusive part of the Eixample. The architect designed an apartment building in accordance with the style of *Modernisme* in vogue at the time, to the extent that the facade might be considered somewhat conventional. Indeed, unsuspecting observers might not even notice that the building is by Gaudí. Only the stone gallery, though treated with a certain degree of moderation, reveals something of the architect's original personality.

The facade consists entirely of rough-hewn ashlars and is the only symmetrical composition in the whole of Gaudí's oeuvre. The rhythm established by the interplay of solid wall and openings is highly balanced, even academic. The ground-floor columns evoke bobbins. The gallery is worthy of especial attention, not only because it enters into space but also by virtue of its ubiquitous ornamentation both in well-sculpted stone and in subtle wrought iron. The mushrooms pay tribute to the owner's favorite hobby.

Some of the balconies are over-dimensioned in response to the architect's will to create imposing volume rather than to functional demands.

The uppermost part of the facade, in the typical *modernista* style, is the most striking, and not simply by virtue of the triumph of the curve. The pulleys, in combination with a protective parapet, are a magnificent example of wrought-iron work heralding the style that would later characterize the facade of Casa Batlló. At the same level, the architect placed the sculpted heads of three personalities closely linked to the personality of the owner, Andreu Calvet: that of Sant Pere Màrtir, in reference to the name of the owner's father; and those of Sant Ginés Notari and Sant Ginés Còmic, the patron saints of Vilassar, Calvet's native town.

When we stand before the front door we already realize that this is no ordinary building. We are told this by the highly personalized plaque surrounding the doorbells and above all by the exceptional knocker. We can tell not only by its size but also by the quality of the wrought-iron work that this is no ordinary piece, but to understand its true significance we must lift the cross-shaped knocker (representing good), which strikes an enormous bed-bug (evil). Having crossed the threshold we enter the foyer, a highly articulated, unspectacular space featuring turned columns, Valencia tiles of characteristic Mediterranean luminosity, decorated ceilings, a bench and mirror designed by the architect, the fretwork casing of a transparent elevator, and the forceful yet aerial banisters, that seem to invite us to climb the stairs. Every detail, even the most insignificant, was designed by Gaudí. Furthermore, the doors to the apartments feature three details I find truly enchanting: the spyhole, like the tiny cells of a beehive; the highly functional mailbox; and the door handle that, despite its innovative design, adapts better to the hand than its more conventional counterparts.

Relatively recently Casa Calvet acquired greater importance in that what had hitherto been a private part of the building has become public. The Restaurant Calvet on the ground floor occupies what were once the offices of the textile industry belonging to the owner. Here Gaudí made everything to measure, from the partitions that separate the different areas to individual chairs and communal benches via the weighty fretwork beam that seems to support everything. It is wonderful to observe the modernity of the beam in relation to the gentle ocher tones covering the walls, in which the presence of brick is no more than a subtle hint. The joinery is of outstanding quality, as is the metalwork and stained glass at the entrance. The Gaudi scholar Joan Bassegoda i Nonell states that the furniture by the prestigious firm of Casas & Bardés is entirely dovetailed, that is, fitted together without the use of nails. While the large stained-glass panel separating the restaurant from the toilets is recent, the ambience created by Gaudí has been preserved. Period photographs allude to the aroma of that time. Framed and hanging on the wall, a reproduction of the poster Antoni Utrillo painted on the occasion of Calvet's Solidaritat candidacy during the 1906 elections: a *modernista* lady addresses the citizens of Catalonia as "my children" and asks them to vote for Calvet i Pintó. The result was an almost unanimous yes vote.

⑪ Forn Sarret
Carrer de Girona 73

Forn de la Concepció
Carrer de Girona 74

Evidence that *modernisme* was perhaps the last 'true' style is the fact that it impregnated many walks of life. The work of the great creators influenced that of more modest decorators and drove even the lowliest shopkeepers to update their establishments. We do not know who designed these two bakeries, which reveal the intensity of an urban landscape that unfortunately has not survived intact. While Forn Sarret is still full of life, the future of the Forn de la Concepción, which closed some years ago, is still very uncertain.

(12) CASES ANTONI ROCAMORA

1917
Passeig de Gràcia 6, 8–10 and 12–14

JOAQUIM AND BONAVENTURA BASSEGODA I AMIGÓ, *architects*

The Casas Antoni Rocamora apartment block was unusual in its day for its large dimensions. It is clearly Frenchified in style, a trend in vogue at the time. The project is strikingly, austerely elegant, a quality enhanced by the use of stone. The roofline is in keeping with this aesthetic, even with its crenellations and glazed ceramic cupolas. The few *modernista* elements are decorative, and are to be found inside.

(13) CASA MANUEL MALAGRIDA
1908
Passeig de Gràcia 27

JOAQUIM CODINA I MATALÍ, *architect*

Manuel Malagrida, having made his fortune in the Americas, returned to Barcelona and commissioned this house, which resembles a family palace in Frenchified style, particularly the attic story. The building is faced with stone. The shop entrances are characterized by half-hidden wrought-iron railings and *modernista* lamps. The heads in the relief are of Christopher Columbus and General Bartolomé Mitre. The most personal element is possibly the cupola, crowned by wrought-iron, the most spectacular in the whole of the *Eixample*. This was the artist Antoni Clavé's first "painting": as a worker at the Tolosa industrial painting firm Clavé he was required to apply a coat of red lead so high up that he almost fainted. He asserts that the original color of the dome, which was lost after the war, was gold.

(14) CASA ALBERT LLEÓ I MORERA

1905
Passeig de Gràcia 35

LLUÍS DOMÈNECH I MONTANER, *architect*

The architect restricted himself to altering the structure of an already existing building, although he endowed it with such a wealth of ornamentation that it became one of the most emblematic examples of *Modernisme*. The people of Barcelona saw such stylistic dissonance with nearby Casa Amatller (Passeig de Gràcia 41) and Casa Batlló (no. 43) that they called the block the *Mançana de la Discòrdia* (apple of discord; *mançana* is the Catalan word for both "apple" and "block"). The feeling was that the block had been designed by the best architects in the world, each one according to his own style.

The ground floor was highly original before its 1943 mutilation, the central attractions being two huge, magnificent sculptures by Arnau: beautiful *modernista* ladies holding fonts which are almost entirely enveloped by the waves of their clothes. The bottom part of the central gallery originally featured sculpted heads by Alfons Juyol. At first-floor level there are four highly avant-garde feminine reliefs representing the technical advances of the time: the phonograph, electricity, photography, and the telephone. Besides other minor decorative elements, the facade was crowned by a small pavilion clad inside with mosaics by Bru.

The interior was even more sumptuously decorated than the exterior. Indeed, the foyer, the staircase leading up to the apartments, and the elevator all reveal that *Modernisme* was a triumph for the decorative arts.

The first floor, on which the owner lived, is truly spectacular. The most outstanding piece here is Arnau's sculptural interpretation of the lullaby "La dida de l'infant del Rei" (The King's Baby's Nanny), which crowns the door arches, although not to be outdone was the furniture, designed by the great joiner Gaspar Homar, which now enriches the Museu d'Art Modern collection. Fortunately, it is still possible to contemplate in this apartment the murals also designed by this great artist, in collaboration with the painter Josep Pey, the sculptor Joan Carreras, the ceramist Antoni Serra, and the mosaicist Mario Maragliano. Equally exceptional is the stained glass panel that closes the circular gallery, a masterpiece designed by Pey and executed by Rigalt & Graner. And also, worthy of special attention are the delicate joinery and marquetry work by Joan Sagarra that in the rooms overlooking the avenue, the fireplace carved by Carreras, and the flooring in the entire dwelling, the work of the Escofet firm.

The house positively overflows with beauty. It is up to the visitor to minutely examine the infinity of details that reveal the high degree of perfection in the work of artisans who ranked among the best in Europe. Furthermore, this dwelling, an exemplary sample of those scattered throughout the *Dreta de l'Eixample*, gives us an accurate idea of the quality lavished by the haute bourgeoisie on their homes.

The generation who immediately succeeded the *modernistas*, the *noucentistes*, hated the preceding style so much that they set out to destroy it. Thus in 1943 the architect Francesc Ferrer i Bartolomé produced a project for the Loewe boutique, which involved mutilating the facade and interior of the ground and mezzanine floors. Since Ferrer was not affiliated to the architectural association, the plans were signed by the outstanding architect Francesc Duran i Reynals, a militant *noucentista*. However, even more atrocities were perpetrated: the roof pavilion was demolished, after having been severely damaged when in 1937 it was used by the FAI anarchists as a machine-gun nest from which to spray the communist PSUC headquarters opposite. The two sculptures by Arnau were neither kept nor sold: they were smashed by hammer blows, explained art historian Josep Gudiol, whose horrified eyes witnessed the atrocity. The concierge, however, managed to salvage the heads. Dalí told me that when he learnt of this, as one of the champions of *Modernisme* he bought the pieces for three thousand pesetas each and encrusted them in the wall of the central patio of his museum in Figueres.

Several decades having passed, Loewe, aware of the errors they committed, agreed to eliminate the funereal decoration that framed their display windows and entrusted Oscar Tusquets with the difficult task of recomposing the ground floor of the building. Tusquets managed to produce something reminiscent of the original, so that those who remember Domènech i Montaner's work might be in a better position to appreciate the efforts made.

(15) Casa Antoni Amatller

1900
Passeig de Gràcia 41

Josep Puig i Cadafalch, *architect*

Puig i Cadafalch's work on Casa Amatller consisted of alterations to an existing build-ing, much like the cases of Domènech i Montaner with Casa Lleó Morera and Gaudí with Casa Batlló. The architect transformed the facade, the foyer, the inner patio, the staircase leading to the owners' residence, and the residence itself into a *modernista* gem.

Antoni Amatller was the proprietor of a prosperous and famed chocolate business. On his death, his daughter, Teresa, continued to live in the apartment, where she cre-ated the Institut d'Art Hispànic. Living as she was on such a prominent, prestigious avenue, she gave the architect free rein to endow the building with the maximum air of distinction.

Puig i Cadafalch drew up a spectacular though moderate project, which according to Alexandre Cirici belongs to his red period, the color he assigns to the architect's *modernista* work. The facade conceals none of Puig i Cadafalch's deliberate wish to reveal his several sources of inspiration, all of which are readily detectable. For exam-ple, the Catalan neo-Gothic of the windows and the neo-Flemish of the gallery; for example, a stretch of wall that seems to have been taken from an eighteenth-century Amsterdam house. What really surprises the observer is the fact that such a variety of origins should exist side by side in harmony, each style enriching the others. This is something that only an architect of the caliber of Puig i Cadafalch could achieve.

The best craftsmen, under the firm hand of their works director, contributed the best of their knowledge and talents. The facade combines subtle, polychrome sgraffiti; wrought-iron work, which heightens the balconies and the door; tiles with reliefs and metallic sheens; fine, delicate stone ornamentation; and the carpentry of doors and windows, originally painted green, as has recently been discovered.

An outstanding element of the facade is the asymmetry of the two adjacent and very different doors, featuring the work of sculptor Eusebi Arnau, who created a daringly innovative Saint George who links the doors in an original way.

The foyer was conceived as a coach entrance. Puig i Cadafalch placed a special kind of paving there, although he used the material, format, and style of the tiles that cover the city's pavements as part of the evident desire to establish a continuum.

At the far end of this space, which though dark and prosaic is nonetheless embellished by much ornamentation, such as lamps and stained glass, stands the inner patio. This open space features the access solution typical of this kind of mansion: an elegant, solemn staircase leading up to the *planta principal* and a simple counterpart providing access to the apartments on the floors above. A large, stained-glass skylight covers the patio.

What was once the residence of the Amatller family has retained all of its original flavor, despite the fact that it was renamed Institut Amatller d'Art Hispànic, the doors of which are open to researchers into the world of art. The offices, at the far end, have scrupulously preserved not only the decor but even the furniture, while the front part contains the collections that Amatller amassed.

The decorative arts are also very generously featured here in the contributions of Arnau, sculpture; Juyol, carved stone; the Franzi broth-ers, marble; Joan Paradís, sgraffiti; Esteve Andorrà and Manuel Ballarín, wrought iron; Masriera i Campins, bronze; Torres Mauri i Pujol and Baucis, ceramics; Casa & Bardés, carpentry; Joan Coll, gypsum work; Escofet, flooring; Mario Maragliano, mosaics; Gaspar Homar, furniture and joinery; Miret i Ascens and Antoni Tàpies, lights.

The restoration work carried out on the occasion of the Olympic Games returned to the facade the original restrained, seignorial elegance it boasted at the turn of the century.

⑯ CASA JOSEP BATLLÓ

1907
Passeig de Gràcia 43

ANTONI GAUDÍ I CORNET, *architect*

Gaudí, commissioned by the textile industrialist Josep Batlló i Casanovas, restricted himself to carrying out an operation similar to that of the adjacent Casa Lleó Morera and Casa Amatller, all of which would soon be christened the Mançana de la Discòrdia. Gaudí was perfectly aware that he had a unique opportunity to create a striking work in keeping with Barcelona's most spectacular setting of the time: Passeig de Gràcia.

The influence of the architect Josep Maria Jujol, who here began his close collaboration with Gaudí, is very evident in the asymmetrical, abstract, free design of the facade, as the architect Carlos Flores has shown in his exhaustive study of the mutually enriching relationship between both. Also contributing was the usual team of skilled artisans, which included the Badia brothers (wrought iron), Casa & Bardés (joinery), Pujol & Baucis (tiling), Ribó (ceramics), and Josep Pelegrí (stained glass). The cladding for the cross and the facade disks came from Manacor.

Much speculation has been made about the symbolism of the facade. Some interpret it as a representation of Carnival (the masks) and confetti (the polychrome ceramics), while others see the evocation of the transparent waters of a cove on the Costa Brava. However, a religious mystic such as Gaudí would never have had recourse to such a pagan theme as Carnival. More likely, this is a highly personal recreation of the legend of Saint George and the dragon: there is the lance (in the form of the circular tower crowned by the three-dimensional cross and highlighted by the initials of the Holy Family); the spine of the dragon's body (the roof crest) with its wound (the hole outlined in red); the animal's skin (the abstract, polychrome treatment of the central part of the facade); skull fragments (the balcony railings) and bones (forms composing the ground and first floors) of the victims devoured by the dragon, piled up in its cave (cavities and openings suggested on these two floors). It is no coincidence that the astonished people of Barcelona christened the building "la Casa dels Ossos" (the House of Bones). They were not far off the mark, for it must be remembered, moreover, that the balcony railings and the grille over the front door were painted pale ocher, instead of the usual black. After the war they were repainted in black; the people had forgotten the color chosen by Gaudí, to the extent that when the building was correctly restored in 1980, some voices were raised in protest against what they considered lack of fidelity.

The almost gestural originality observable in this work marks a radical break from Gaudí's previous Barcelona style. Furthermore, the tachiste abstraction Jujol applied to the facade is astonishingly avant-garde. When the early-morning sun rakes onto the wall, the glazed ceramics and the fragments of glass used in this composition acquire a highly gratifying luminosity. Jujol used the ceramic disks left over for the gigantic serpentine bench in the Park Güell.

The most striking element of the foyer is its luminous surfaces, which, in the patio, become lighter further down the wall, in order better to reflect the natural light that filters in from above. The elevator is a remarkable piece of work.

From the vestibule the wooden staircase leads up to the first floor. For the staircase, the architect created a joinery covering reminiscent of the spinal column of the dragon.

The subtle reliefs of the doors and the cave-fire-place-bench are possibly the most striking elements in an ensemble every detail of which is essential. It is a shame that almost nothing remains of the former splendor, the oratory having been removed as well as the furniture, which was on occasions deprived of adequate light, such as that from the dining-room ceiling. Although we can no longer appreciate the design of the chairs, there is a story behind them worth telling. Gaudí asked Batlló's wife how many men and women there were in the family, but before replying she wanted to know why. When she learnt that the idea was to create a different model for each sex, she flew into a rage. Gaudí had no option but to create a unisex model. (Different models for men and women, however, would have been in keeping with the fashions of the time.)

The attic is worth a visit, by virtue of the spatial form created by the rhythm of parabolic arches. The visitor should also savor the flat roof or *terrat*, where it is possible to touch the dragon's sensual ceramic spinal column and the chimneys covered in *trencadís*. Neither should the rear facade be overlooked, in which it is possible to detect the typical structure of the block of apartments, although Gaudí framed it with the same cladding of fragments of ceramic. Some details should be noted, such as the simple though telling railings and the remains of the ornamentation of the wall separating the building from the one next door.

(17) Editorial Montaner i Simon
1880
Carrer d'Aragó 255

Lluís Domènech i Montaner, *architect*

The new offices for the publisher Editorial Montaner i Simon that were completed in 1888 heralded the *Modernisme* that was approaching, and it is no coincidence that it was designed by an architect who would be the movement's cornerstone. (Gaudí, by virtue of his genius, must be considered a case apart.) Despite his youth, Domènech was given this commission thanks to family ties, since one of the publishers was his brother.

The building, which today houses the Fundació Antoni Tàpies, is restrained and austere, in keeping with its original commercial function. The observer notices that the surface devoted to openings is far greater than that given over to structure: the architect wanted the offices to be illuminated as far as possible by natural light. Of the three basic materials used for the exterior—iron, glass, and red brick—the latter assumes the leading role, further evidence of the neo-Mudéjar influence that guided the architect's hand in the form of certain openings and the brilliant use of flat brick. The

busts and the names inscribed on the crest, the only decorative concessions, pay homage to the world of literature.

The incipient *Modernisme* of the facade is detected in the first *coup de fouet* to appear in Barcelona, the four railings that protect the semi-basement, and also in the brick, which is proudly displayed rather than hidden behind false claddings that imitate stone or stucco that imitates cobbles, characteristic of the eclecticism then in vogue. Neither did Domènech i Montaner attempt to conceal the structure, which is visible all over the facade. This is why the layout of the open-plan interior is based on the transparency of space, thanks to the use of numerous cast-iron pillars, elements that the architect also leaves visible. Oriol Bohigas has said that this is the first building in Catalonia to come close to architectural rationalism.

Another striking element of the interior, apart from the cast-iron columns, is the use of glass, some of which is stained, and of polygonal decorative motifs evocative of certain aspects of Arab architecture.

This publishing house continued to function until the early 1970s, a time when Barcelonans were rediscovering an appreciation for this industrial facade that, thanks to the creativity of Domènech i Montaner, was in no way out of place in one of the noblest parts of the *Eixample*.

When the business closed, Antoni Tàpies had the fortunate idea of transforming the premises into the foundation that bears his name. Architects Roser Amadó and Lluís Domènech i Girbau, great-grandson of the *modernista* master, carried out the refurbishing project. While they were scrupulously respectful of the facade, inside they worked with absolute freedom, highlighting a number of ornamental details, such as display cases, pillars and, above all, the shelves designed by Domènech i Montaner himself. Most exciting of all, however, was the rediscovery of the open-plan floor, made possible thanks to the dozens of cast-iron pillars.

An avant-garde sculpture made to measure by Tàpies, a piece resembling a gestural drawing that stands out against the sky, crowned by the outline of a chair (which in Tàpies's world of images evokes thought and reflection),

fulfills the two-fold mission of filling the ugly void between the two adjoining buildings and at the same time of advertising in a very striking way the public institution that houses his art.

(18) CASA DOLORS CALM

1903
Rambla de Catalunya 54

JOSEP VILASECA I CASANOVAS, *architect*

In 1903 Josep Vilaseca, the prestigious architect whose major work to that point had been the 1888 Universal Exposition's Arc de Triomf, was commissioned to make alterations to an existing building in the form of a new facade and interior decor. The most original aspect of this work is the vertical gallery, with its crucial joinery work. Each floor features a different design, while the openings are embellished with suggestive stained glass. Visitors must look up so as not to miss the decoration scattered all over the facade and even on the bottom part of the gallery. The polychrome sgraffiti that covers the facade and the floral motif sculptural reliefs on the window tympanums reveal a deep horror vacui. The first floor still preserves its original sumptuous *modernista* decoration.

The nineteenth-century facade of what used to be a prestigious hatter on Carrer Ferran ("Prats is quality" wrote Joan Miró on a drawing-collage) was entirely transposed to its new site and later sensitively converted into that of the present-day Galeria Joan Prats.

The ornate roofline was spoiled by the addition of several extra floors.

⑲ Casa doctor Miquel A. Fargas

1904
Rambla de Catalunya 47

Enric Sagnier i Villavecchia, *architect*

The elegant Sagnier here displays his French-style *Modernisme*. The subtle, restrained ornamentation appears only at strategic points, while the building as a whole is a model of austerity. Outstanding features are the wrought-iron work on the main gallery and the mezzanine floor windows. The porter's lodge is worth a visit by virtue of its balance and its two *modernista* joinery pieces: the banisters and, above all, the mirror.

⟨20⟩ Farmàcia Bolós

1901
Rambla de Catalunya 77 / Carrer de València 256

Antoni and J. M. de Falguera i Sivilla, *architects*

This is the most important of the *modernista* pharmacies. Despite its small size, it produces a strong impact on the unwary customer.

The work was commissioned before family ties were established, when the client married the architects' sister, Carme Falguera. While the exterior was embellished by the stained-glass door, featuring an orange tree laden with ripe fruit, the interior was a delicate, striking ensemble much of which has been preserved to this day. The owner, Antoni Novellas i Roig, described the decor in his diary:

"These friends designed the pharmacy, in accordance with the neo-modern style then in vogue, taking maximum advantage of a small space in poor condition. The laboratory was reduced to a salon-dispensary, with large polychrome stained-glass grilles featuring an orange tree, looking onto the street. The shelves were of red beechwood and the studiedly whimsical counter of beech, ash, and mahogany. The decor was symbolic in style. The vaulted ceiling featured two friezes of leaves and botanical motifs against a bluish background, the corners finished with four gilt and green medallions, with the chalice and the serpent, beneath which there were ribbons with the names of Fors, Carbonell, Scheele, and Loewery, four great pharmacists who deserve my respect. The botanical motif that linked the four medallions, based on poppies, thorn-apples, henbane, aconites, and primulas, was on the panel at the far end, with two ephebes pounding drugs in a large mortar, while the sun rose in the sky heralding the cool splendor of the new day."

Bravo!

Novellas sold his business to Antoni de Bolós i Vayreda, who subsequently passed it down to his son, Jordi Bolós i Capdevila, the latest in the line of fourteen generations of pharmacists.

21 CASA EVARIST JUNCOSA

1909
Rambla de Catalunya, 78

SALVADOR VIÑALS I SABATER, *architect*

Symmetry once reigned here, since the house next door (no. 76) was an identical project by the same architect for the same owner, which reveals the extent of the mutilations that building has suffered. Above a surface whose texture is obtained through the use of irregular, rough-hewn ashlars, there is a large tympanum decorated with plant motif reliefs. The porter's lodge features interesting *modernista* decoration (above all on the doorbell panel). Here we find the base of the elaborate staircase leading to the owner's first-floor apartment and that of the more prosaic stairs for the other residents. The stairwell is enclosed by fine stained-glass panels.

(22) Casa Josep i Ramon Queraltó

1907
Rambla de Catalunya 88 / Carrer de Mallorca 249

Josep Plantada i Artigas, *architect*

Casa Josep i Ramon Queraltó suffered a mutilation some years ago in which some fine architectural features were removed, including pinnacles and an angular turret at the top and pergolas on the corners of the first floor. The sgraffiti, which decorates the whole of the recently restored facade, and the stone carvings over tribunes of the second floor, are the best remaining features of the original project.

(23) Casa Enric Batlló

1896
Passeig de Gràcia 75 / Mallorca 259 and 263

Josep Vilaseca i Casanovas, *architect*

The author of the Arc de Triomf designed this apartment complex for a client who had three daughters, which explains, perhaps, why the project consists of three independent buildings. Vilaseca's work is an example of how some *modernista* architects contributed to fostering the decorative arts. Although a number of artisans were involved, we know for certain only that the wrought iron is by Sancristòfol and the ceramics by the firm of Pujol & Bausis. The facade establishes an attractive dialogue between high-quality stone, bare brick, and glazed ceramic. Between the first-floor windows was placed a series of fine ceramic coats of arms with metallic finish. The balcony of the floor above is graced by subtle wrought-iron work. Other outstanding decorative elements on the top floor are the floral motif ceramic panels. The conversion of the building on the corner into the Hotel Condes de Barcelona prompted the restoration of the facade.

(24) THIRTY-TWO BENCH-LAMPPOSTS
1906
Passeig de Gràcia

PERE FALQUÉS I URPÍ, *architect*

Besides being a highly competent architect, Pere Falqués proved to be the best lamppost designer of his time. Having festooned the Saló de Sant Joan (Passeig Lluís Companys), he created this exquisite model that was put in place on December 26, 1906.

What a Christmas gift! The wrought-iron work centered on this vibrant *coup de fouet* that runs like lightning down the whole length of the lamppost was produced at the prestigious Ballarín workshop. The *trencadís* bench lost its functionality when it was subjected to unfortunate alterations in the 1960s.

In 1909 Falqués placed more fantastic lampposts in the Cinc d'Oros (at the crossroads with Avinguda Diagonal), which today stand on the Avinguda de Gaudí.

㉕ CASA JAUME FORN

1909
Carrer de Roger de Llúria 52 / Carrer de València 285

JERONI F. GRANELL I MANRESA, *architect*

One of the decorative arts that enjoyed spectacular prosperity thanks to *Modernisme* was that of painting with light, that is, stained glass. The most interesting aspect of this facade is precisely the set of stained-glass windows that decorate the vertical galleries of glass and wrought iron. The style of these windows suggests that they are probably the work of the prestigious firm of Rigalt & Granell, although there is no documentary evidence to support this. The semi-cylindrical column that highlights the corner arris is a legacy of eclecticism.

26 CASA VIUDA DE MARFÀ

1905
Passeig de Gràcia 66 / Carrer de València 274

MANUEL COMAS I THOS, *architect*

This is a fine example of neo-Gothic *Modernisme*, the spectacular quality of which was
enhanced by the building's location on a corner of Passeig de Gràcia. Outstanding features of the almost symmetrical facade are the purity of the main gallery, which
belongs more to the exterior than to the dwelling, and the smaller galleries, which
appear to be almost literally suspended in space. The stone ornamentation is the work
of Alfons Juyol. While the front door remains closed, the counterpoint of fine wood
endows the ground floor with elegance; on the other hand, when it is open, the three
arches reveal the solemnity of a vestibule designed as a coach entrance from which the
magnificent staircase rises and leads to the first-floor residence of the owner.

(27) MUNICIPAL CONSERVATORY

1916
Carrer del Bruc 104–112 / Carrer de València 330

ANTONI DE FALGUERA, *architect*

Originally designed to be a school for deaf mutes, in 1911 it was decided to convert the building into a conservatory. The architect Falguera, in collaboration with his colleagues Florensa and Vilaseca, made the necessary modifications to the project. The conservatory was not officially opened until 1926.

The exterior is of an almost Nordic austerity, neither does its neo-Gothic air seem to bear any relation to the predominant style of the time, although here it is possible to detect an approach similar to that of certain works by Puig i Cadafalch, such as Casa Terrades (Casa de les Punxes). Perhaps the origin of the brief influenced the architect, who had already created the Casa de la Lactància, on the Gran Via, which revealed his capacity to relate more directly to *Modernisme*, even in terms of the decorative arts.

The basic materials used were stone and brick, with ceramic tile on the roof.

The openings are the minimum necessary to fulfill their function, and verticality pervades. The most outstanding elements are the semifreestanding cylindrical towers, strategically situated to resolve the corners. The four figures that frame the coat of arms of the city of Barcelona, which crowns the main door, are by Arnau and contrast with the prevailing austerity. The theme of the rolled parchment appears in the adornment of some windows and the door capitals. The other exterior concession consists of the panels decorated with polychrome mosaics, featuring the coats of arms of the city and of Catalonia, while the other two are characterized by the lyre and floral details.

The interior is far from spectacular, although it is rich in decorative details: the ceramic or marble handrails; sgraffiti; finely sculpted stone capitals; good joinery work. The most outstanding element, however, is the so-called *Peixera* (fishbowl), with its fine stained glass. The large oval skylight is also worthy of mention, although it is more *noucentista* than *modernista*.

㉘ CASA MANUEL LLOPIS
1903
Carrer de València 339

ANTONI GALLISSÀ I SOQUÉ, *architect;* J. M. JUJOL, *collaborating architect*

Once again the street corner high-lights this building, Gallissà's most outstanding work. An astonishing dialogue is set up between a brick ground floor with arcades and a white facade whose rhythm is quite different. The verticality of the galleries accentuates what has been described as an air reminiscent of the Alhambra. Here Jujol drew a number of personal sgraffiti, which act as a counterpoint to an otherwise restrained facade. It is a shame that the crowning element was mutilated. The Arderiu pharmacy, which harmonizes so well with the ensemble, is worth a visit. The whole building is a valuable personal contribution to *Modernisme*.

(29) CASA JOSEP THOMAS
1898
Carrer de Mallorca 291–293

LLUÍS DOMÈNECH I MONTANER, *architect*
FRANCESC GUÀRDIA I VIAL, *architect* (1912)

The history of this building may be divided into two highly differentiated phases.

The first, in which the industrialist Josep Thomas commissioned a house that would meet his professional and family needs. This is the reason there are two entrances framed by a gigantic void, which beneath a depressed arch allowed the natural light to filter through into the workshop. Thomas's lithography and photogravure studio was possibly the most prestigious at the time and closely associated with the *modernista* adventure in the graphic arts, since it published, among others, Ramon Casas's magazines *4 Gats* and *Pèl & Ploma*. While one of the doors led to the business, the other led to the stairs that climbed up to the owner's residence, which occupied the whole of the first floor and the two side towers, one of which was crowned by a stone pinnacle featuring the wrought-iron sign advertising the establishment.

The facade decoration is based on grilles and stained-glass panels, protecting the great central opening; the continuous stone parapet on the first floor; and the glazed tiles and buttons with a metallic sheen adorned with heraldic elements, one of Domènech i Montaner's confessed passions.

In 1912 the architect's son-in-law, Francesc Guàrdia, designed a model extension to the building. He added three floors, stitching the addition to the original building by means of two end galleries. The top

floor eatured columns that entered into a dialogue on an equal footing with those of the first floor, and the whole building was crowned with the same profile as the original one. Unfortunately, practically no other intervention of this kind in Barcelona has been carried out with such respect and creativity.

In 1979 a further intervention took place that might have mutilated the building, although the end result was positive. The design firm BD occupied what had originally been Thomas's workshop, and commissioned architect Cristian Cirici of Estudi Per to carry out the necessary alterations. Cirici's project was also respectful and sacrificed only the absolute minimum.

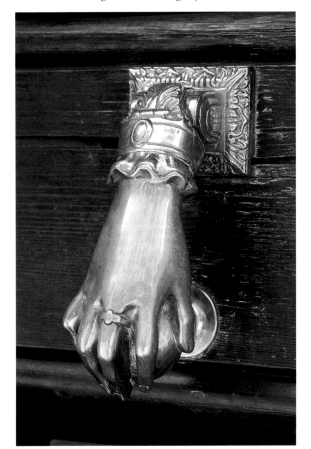

(30) PALAU RAMON MONTANER
1893
Carrer de Mallorca 278

LLUÍS DOMÈNECH I MONTANER, *architect*

Josep Domènech i Estapà was originally commissioned to build this palace, and it was he who drew up the plans. However, when work was already in progress, disagreements arose between architect and client, which ended in a breaking-off of relations. Ramon Montaner then turned to Lluís Domènech i Montaner, to whom he was related on his mother's side. The ground floor and two floors above had been completed, as had the wall and the design of the railings. Domènech therefore built the third floor and the sumptuous interior and exterior decoration.

The palace was surrounded by a much larger garden, to the extent that together with what his partner Simon (Editorial Montaner i Simon) had ordered to be built several years previously (and demolished a few decades ago), both buildings occupied the whole of Carrer de Mallorca between Carrer de Roger de Llúria and Carrer de Pau Claris.

The most outstanding elements of the facades is the ornamentation: large panels of glazed tiles with the symbols of the firm and of the inventor of the printing press. Beneath the eaves of the facade overlooking Carrer Mallorca appears the stone relief of the eagle framed by two coats of arms, in which appears the year of the building's completion.

The interior decor is for the most part studiedly palatial: in the foyer, on the main staircase and in the main hall proliferate sculpted reliefs, fine joinery work, and mosaics—all of which reveal Domènech i Montaner's passion for heraldry as an ornamental motif. Among those who worked as part of his team were Eusebi Arnau, the stone carver Becchini, the stained-glass maker Antoni Rigalt, the joiner Gaspar Homar, and the carpenter Planas i Tort.

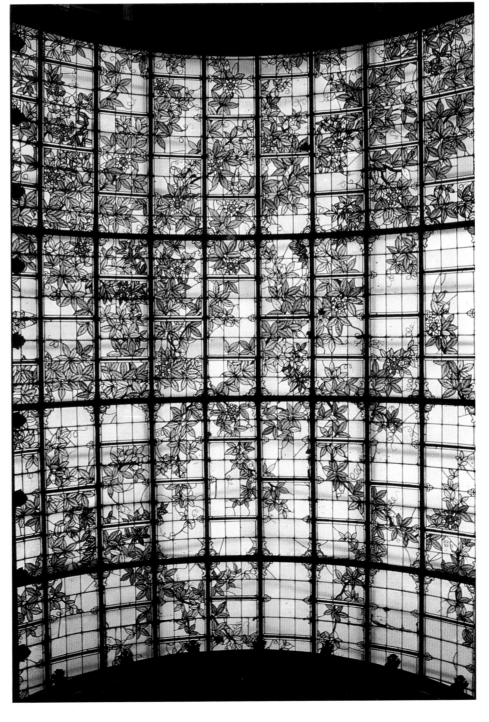

③ Casa Pere Milà

1910
Passeig de Gràcia 92 / Carrer de Provença 261–265

Antoni Gaudí i Cornet, *architect*

La Pedrera is the genius's greatest secular work, his religious masterpiece being the church of the Colònia Güell. Furthermore, La Pedrera is more than just an architectural masterpiece; it is a sculpture.

Pere Milà i Camps married in second nuptials Roser Guardiola, the widow of the rich *indià* José Guardiola i Grau. It was Milà's friend and partner, Josep Batlló, who recommended Gaudí as the architect for the large apartment block he intended to build. Milà decided to overlook the fact that Gaudí was very expensive, since he loved to improvise and often made his workers rebuild everything he did not like, and gave him free rein to create anything he wanted (with one exception, noted below). The result speaks highly eloquently for itself.

Several specialists have suggested different natural sources of inspiration for the building. Some assure us that it is Calescobes, on Menorca; others, Fra Guerau, in the mountains of Prades; or Sant Miquel del Fai, in the Vallès region; or the mountain of Pareis, on Mallorca; the novelist Juan Goytisolo has even suggested distant Cappadocia. My opinion, however, is that his source of inspiration was the crest of Sant Sadurní, which he discovered during his long sojourn in Sant Felíu de Codines and which looms over the small village of Gallifa (Vallès Occidental).

Whatever the case, La Pedrera is a personal recreation of a stony massif, with its bushes (the balcony handrails), crowned by the suggestion of clouds (the change in color and form of the attics). All this was originally to have been the gigantic pedestal for a sculpture of the Virgin and Child. When the astonished people of Barcelona saw the building for the first time, they appropriately christened it La Pedrera (the Quarry).

This work marks the sublimation of the curve, a strategy highly characteristic of *Modernisme*. And not only on the facade, for the same rhythms are repeated inside. Consequently it need not surprise us that when Maeght was weighing up the possibility of opening a gallery in Barcelona, one of the venues he considered was the first floor of La Pedrera, which at the time served as a bingo hall. However, he had to dismiss the idea due to the lack of flat surfaces, a serious problem when it comes to hanging pictures, especially bearing in mind that the French gallery owner's intention was to respect and enhance Gaudí's work.

La Pedrera was conceived as a free structure, in which the bearing walls are rings concentric to the exterior and interior facades of the patios. Consequently, as long as the columns are respected, the layout of each floor can be modified or even completely transformed (as the Caixa Catalunya, owner of the building, has done by converting the first floor into an exhibitions hall). The formal richness of the exterior rhythm is truly impressive, with interplay between curves, cavities, and voids. The architect Josep Maria Jujol, Gaudí's closest collaborator, was given absolute freedom to create the balcony handrails, and the result is a major avant-garde work, fruit of improvisation that pays homage to gestural art. Jujol improvised them in the founder's workshop. The people of Barcelona were truly astounded when they saw the completed facade. As soon as Jujol's work had been completed, two Catalan sculptors, Pau Gargallo and Julio González, discovered that it was possible to use iron in sculpture, and they were the first to do so.

The skin of La Pedrera has an unfinished texture reminiscent of the last works of Michelangelo, obtained once the huge stone blocks, obtained from the quarries of Garraf and dressed by a legion of masons, had been fitted together.

The wrought-iron doors, designed by Gaudí, open into two huge interior patios in which the space, enriched by polychrome, also bears the imprint of Gaudí. The original design of the staircase, which led up to the Milàs' residence, contrasts curiously with the rather pedestrian elevator. Neither did Gaudí have anything to do with the paintings in the foyer: Aleix Clapés, without consulting the architect, chose the themes and engaged Xavier Nogués, Iu Pasqual, and Teresa Lostau (who were more to the owner's tastes) to paint them under almost slavelike conditions. As if this were not enough, the owner's wife took a thorough dislike to Gaudí, and took advantage of the architect's accidental death to destroy the entire interior decor and replace it with a new one in pseudo–Louis XV style.

As I mentioned earlier, the building was conceived as a gigantic pedestal to support a sculpture of the Virgin. Carles Mani produced a small scale model of the piece, but the Milàs hated it. This is the true reason why it was never placed, not the owners' supposed fear that revolutionaries might one day set fire to the house. Perhaps it is just as well that the sculpture never went beyond the project stage, for to judge from the drawing made some years later by Matamala, the academicism of the sculpture would have been thoroughly out of keeping with the rest of the building.

Such a building needed to be crowned with something in tune with the circumstances, and so it was. The normally prosaic chimneys, stairwells, and ventilators on the flat roof were transformed by Gaudí into creative forms, raising them to the category of artworks that were pioneers of abstraction.

What was originally the attic, reserved for the washrooms, has been restored recently by Caixa Catalunya, since in the 1950s it was converted into a set of penthouse apartments by the architect Barba Corsini. It is still a wonder that a structure of brick can be so creative, even viewed from today's perspective of greater sensitivity to humble materials.

When the work had been completed, a municipal functionary rightly decided that it contravened building regulations, and it was feared that it might be mutilated. The case was resolved thanks to the foresight of the city council, who recognized its exceptional quality and granted permission.

Since it has been the property of Caixa Catalunya, that entity has carried out the laudable task of restoring of the whole building. During the course of the operation, Jujol's ceilings on the first and mezzanine floors were recovered, as were the columns that he himself sculpted in a tour de force of sensitivity. In 1984 UNESCO declared La Pedrera a World Heritage Site.

(32) CASA RAMON CASAS
1899
Passeig de Gràcia 96

ANTONI ROVIRA I RABASSA, *architect*

The painter Ramon Casas was a wealthy man, hence he could afford to build this house and the neighboring one at no. 94, designed by the same architect. Casas lived on the first floor, while his intimate friend Santiago Rusiñol occupied one of the other apartments until his death. The facade is entirely of stone and the repetition of the windows sets up an elegant rhythm, balanced by the sculptural work that culminates the facade. An outstanding element is the long fretwork parapet on the first-floor balcony. The front door, one of the finest in the *Eixample*, opens to reveal a sumptuous foyer with exquisite wrought-iron railings and a staircase that leads up to what was Casas's residence. This apartment may be visited, since it now forms part of the Vinçon home-furnishings emporium. The whole of the decor is the work of the decorator Josep Pascó in collaboration with the Flinch brothers firm of blacksmiths and the ceramist Josep Orriols.

(33) Casa Pere Serra i Pons
1908
Rambla de Catalunya 126

Josep Puig i Cadafalch, *architect*

For reasons unknown, the owner never came to dwell in this single-family residence, which less than a year after it was completed was acquired by an order of nuns, who converted it into a school. This is why there are no outstanding details in the interior.

With this work Puig i Cadafalch paid personal homage to the Palau Gralla in the Old Town (Portaferrissa/Duc de la Victòria), possibly Barcelona's last example of secular Renaissance architecture, which during the mid-nineteenth-century was demolished as part of a deplorable speculative operation. Hence the plateresque adornment of the front door, sculpted by Eusebi Arnau in imitation of the original. Arnau was also responsible for the medallions and coats of arms. Each window also constitutes a homage, in the form of Alfons Juyol's sculpted heads of Cervantes, Wagner, and Mariano Fortuny.

The whole facade is finely carved in stone. The cylindrical tower, a smaller version of those of the Casa de les Punxes, links the two bodies of the building, in which it is possible to detect allusions to national architecture, typical in the work of Puig i Cadafalch.

In 1940, and with the approval of the architect, a colleague of his drew up the plans for a rather unfortunate extension. This was the part demolished when, in 1983, it was acquired by the Barcelona county council as part of a maneuver of real-estate speculation that threatened the very survival of the house. The architect Federico Correa preserved what was worth keeping and integrated the building into a modern, highly respectful complex.

(34) CASA LLUÍS PÉREZ SAMANILLO
1910
Avinguda Diagonal 502–504 / Carrer de Balmes 169

JOAN HERVÀS I ARIZMENDI, *architect*

Joan Hervàs i Arizmendi built Lluís Pérez Samanillo's sumptuous single-family residence in a Frenchified *modernista* style. Although this is by no means obvious, the house has been the victim of mutilations, such as the destruction of the side garden, where the front door originally stood. What I like most about the facade is the *peixera* (fishbowl), the building's most *modernista* element, which looks onto La Diagonal. The fact that since 1947 the house has been the seat of the Círculo Ecuestre has given this urban belvedere even greater importance, since it accommodates the main salon. The crowning medallion featured a sculptural relief of the heart of Jesus, which during the Civil War fell victim to the hammer.

The rich original interior decor has been largely preserved. This work, featuring a large amount of joinery, was directed by the furniture maker Joan Esteva. One of the most outstanding pieces is the large (8-by-3.5 meter) polychrome stained-glass panel that adorns the staircase. This panel was the work of the French brothers J. and E.

Mauméjean. Also worthy of attention are the almost sculptural elevator and the leaded stained-glass door leading into the president's office. Major elements on the ground floor are the former salon, with the marble staircase, and what was the dining room, today the Saló dels Reis, with the aforementioned peixera and its ceiling decorated with painted nymphs. The flooring is of subtle geometrical marquetry.

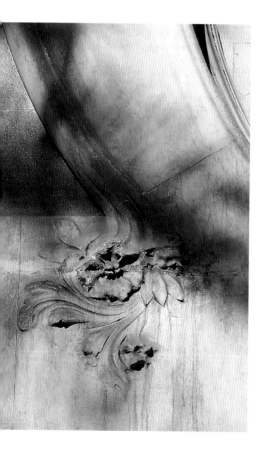

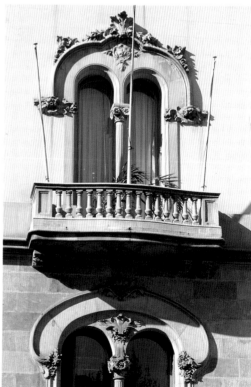

(35) CASA MIQUEL SAYRACH

1918
Avinguda Diagonal 423–425 / Carrer d'Enric Granados 157–159

MANUEL SAYRACH, *architect*

Most historians consider this to be the last *modernista* house. Sayrach, who designed it for his father, was an architect of great personality who set out to build a world of his own imagining. Hence his commissions were few and his output was unfortunately very small. He also designed the house next door, at no. 155 Enric Granados.

The whole stone facade is of high quality—elegant, balanced, and austere. Its most outstanding characteristic is the row of bonelike galleries, which mark the ends of the facade, and the gallery which, like a cylindrical, semi-eccentric column, acts as a hinge between the two bodies of the building. But it is in the attic that a certain affinity with Gaudí can be observed in the form of curves, voids, forms, and even a certain touch of ocher. The whole building is crowned at the central angle by a conical dome.

The formal austerity that predominates over the facade is offset by a genuine horror vacui in the foyer, where the visitor is dazzled by ornamental exuberance. The quality of the furnishings is surpassed only by their marvelous formal originality. The ceilings, walls, staircase, banisters, and elevator are all the result of exquisite design.

(36) CASA BONAVENTURA FERRER

1906
Passeig de Gràcia 113

PERE FALQUÉS I URPÍ , *architect*

Falqués's style, with spectacular volumes that endow his facades with a gigantic air, here reveals its best qualities. While the door, the subtle wrought-iron work on the balconies, and the scenographic crest are some of the outstanding aspects of this facade, what strikes me as more important is the sculptural concept that informs the ground and first floors. Indeed, the large void combined with the gallery just above is a highly personal lesson in balance and forcefulness, in the counterpoint between filled and empty spaces. Now owned by the Deutsche Bank next door, the building has been preserved intact, but remains closed.

37 Casa Marià Fuster i Fuster

1911
Passeig de Gràcia 132

Lluís Domènech i Montaner, *architect*

Casa Fuster is the last urban work by Domènech i Montaner, who took full advantage of the expressive, almost epic, possibilities offered him by the top end of Passeig de Gràcia. Not only is this building the simple culmination of the most seignorial public space of Barcelona, it constitutes a kind of backdrop in the center of the field of vision where the avenue narrows. The maturity of the architect is very apparent here: the building synthesizes all his language and wisdom. The semi-freestanding cylindrical tower at the corner links and heightens the two asymmetrical wall stretches of the facade; it is a shame that the dome conceived to crown the building was never completed. The stone is heightened by pink and white marble, which some historians have associated with Venetian palaces. The ground floor has been restored to its original richness. The owners, the electrical company ENHER, who wanted to demolish the building in the 1960s, recently realized that it is of exceptional emblematic value, a fact that favored its restoration and its conversion into a space open to public activities.

Although the rear facade, which looks over the narrow Carrer de Gràcia, might easily be overlooked, it must be contemplated with attention. Here Domènech i Montaner displayed all his skill by remaining faithful to his style while adapting it to the demands of the surroundings. Indeed, although he made no use of volume here, he managed to maintain in two dimensions all the richness of the composition that distinguishes the other facades.

The *planta principal*, which was the Fuster family residence, has also been restored and is now devoted to social functions.

(38) Casa Comalat

1911
Avinguda Diagonal 442 and Carrer de Còrsega 316 (rear facade)

Salvador Valeri i Pupurull, *architect*

Salvador Valeri was a talented architect; unfortunately, he did not produce much work, but we do have the Casa Comalat at least, a highly original and attractive building. While the forms of the historicizing mezzanine balconies attract attention, the crest of the facade is of a spectacular quality characteristic of *Modernisme*, evoking as it does a highly personal interpretation of a harlequin's hat. The enormous oval fretwork medallion on which it rests has intrigued the citizens of Barcelona, many of whom see it as an allusion to the four stripes of the Catalan flag. This is doubtful, since at the time when it was executed there was enough freedom of expression not to have to turn to this kind of euphemism. This interpretation may have arisen a posteriori, since there has been no lack of anti-Catalan dictatorships in Spain. Carved stone frames the gallery, while fine garlands hang from the top floor.

The most original aspect of the building, however, is the rear facade, an avant-garde ensemble overlooking Carrer de Còrsega, an unusual corner of which the architect took full advantage. Here curves and undulations reign, obtained on the ground floor through the use of stone that evokes fine organic forms that create large voids. Blinds do the rest, and the main ornamental role is played by polychrome ceramic in the form of horizontal panels offset by the verticality of the large frontal crest at the top of the facade, the oxeye window in the center of the crest seems almost postmodern.

③⑨ Palau Baró de Quadras
1906
Avinguda Diagonal 373 / Carrer del Rosselló 279

Josep Puig i Cadafalch, *architect*

The baron of Quadras, satisfied with Josep Puig i Cadafalch's alterations to his family seat in Massanet de la Selva, decided to commission the same architect to design an ostentatious mansion in Barcelona. The Baron had acquired a site overlooking two streets in what was then the incipient Avinguda Diagonal. The dimensions of the site guaranteed that the house would be spectacularly visible.

Like Casa Lleó i Morera, Casa Amatller, and Casa Batlló in the *Mançana de la Discòrdia*, this project was restricted to the transformation of an already existing building, the intense operation affecting basically the foyer and the *planta principal*, where the client would live. The facade is a highly personal synthesis of the Gothic, Mudéjar, and *modernista* styles which, despite its diversity, is an example of the architect's skill in achieving harmonious, sensitive combinations. The main role is played by the gallery running the whole width, heightened by almost plateresque ornamentation, the most outstanding element of which is a sculpture by Arnau depicting Saint George and the dragon. Situated on the corner of the gallery, this work had to be placed in an unusual position with Saint George directly above the beast. The counterpoint to the gallery is the Nordic roofline, featuring steeply sloping dormers with timber gables.

Through highly elegant wrought-iron railings, access is gained to the foyer, in which the banisters, lamps, stucco, stained glass, and Roman mosaic flooring create an exceptionally refined ensemble.

Despite the fact that for decades the palace has housed the Museu de la Música, it has suffered absolutely no mutilations, so visitors may enter and get an idea of how high society lived in those days.

The rear facade, overlooking Carrer del Rosselló, is delicate and harmonious, in the style of the *Eixample*. Polychrome sgraffiti with floral motifs cover the vault of a tribune.

(40) CASA BARTOMEU TERRADES I BRUTAU

1905
Avinguda Diagonal 416–420 / Carrer del Rosselló 260–262

JOSEP PUIG I CADAFALCH, *architect*

Casa Bartomeu Terrades i Brutau is the most striking building not only of the *Eixample* but also of *Modernisme*. The fact that the site was a block of reduced dimensions allowed the owner to acquire the whole plot. The building's unitary appearance is the result of the fact that it was divided among Terrades's three daughters, Rosa, Pepeta, and Àgata. The architect endowed the project with a grandiloquent air and took full advantage of all the benefits of the site, such as the possibility of creating a facade open to the four winds. Given its appearance, the people of Barcelona, always ready with popular names, christened the building la Casa de les Punxes (the House of Thorns).

Puig i Cadafalch drew up a project that in some ways follows the same lines as Casa Amatller, by virtue of its Nordic medieval look, particularly on the crest. The basic material used was red brick, combined with ocher Calafell stone. Despite everything, the facade is rather austere, the three vertical, minutely carved stone galleries fulfilling the mission of breaking the monotony. The most outstanding decorative elements are the enormous polychrome ceramic panels, one of which was the cause of a political controversy. The one at the top of the Carrer Rosselló facade features Saint George and the dragon with the following legend: "Sant Patró de Catalunya torneu-nos la llibertat" (Patron saint of Catalonia, give us back our freedom). The deputy Alejandro Lerroux, a professional demagogue, published a highly aggressive article in the press in which he described this as a "crime against the nation." Wrought-iron work embellishes the balcony railings.

The following craftsmen worked under instructions from Puig i Cadafalch: Alfons Juyol, who was responsible for the stone sculpture; Manuel Ballarín, for the wrought iron; the painter and decorator Enric Monserdà i Vidal, for the interior decor; Eudald Serra for the stained glass; and Masriera & Campins for the brass.

(41) Casa Romá Macaya i Gibert

1901
Passeig de Sant Joan 108

Josep Puig i Cadafalch, *architect*

An important, small single-family palace, Casa Macaya was built on the edge of the *Dreta de l'Eixample*, where the haute bourgeoisie had their new residences built and creative rivalry thrived between not only architects but also proprietors. Puig i Cadafalch built this palace almost simultaneously with Casa Amatller, this being the reason why sculptor Eusebi Arnau carved a capital over the front door, featuring a gentleman mounted on a bicycle. This was a somewhat jocular allusion to the architect, who used this means of transport to visit the works.

White stucco predominates on the facade, serving as a backdrop to the colored sgraffiti and the ocher stone. Above all the minute fretwork by Juyol graces the balcony parapet. The rhythm characterizing the bottom part of the facade is reminiscent of that of Casa Batlló, as is the asymmetrical gallery, with its stone ornamentation. The crest, however, is different, more closely linked to Barcelona's architectural past. The same might be said of the foyer and the large, elegant interior patio from which a solemn staircase rises. This ensemble constitutes the architect's personal homage to the medieval Barcelonan palace. Both these spaces and the interior of the dwelling were sumptuously decorated. Unfortunately, after the Civil War the building housed a school for the deaf and dumb, which led to the interior being greatly altered. Furthermore, the needs of the Caixa Catalunya, which later installed an exhibition hall here, also contributed to the alterations, although the entity correctly restored the facade.

Here follow the names of the main artists and craftsmen who endowed Casa Macaya with such elegance: Arnau, sculpture; Alfons Juyol, carved stone; Joan Paradís, sgraffiti; Pujol & Baucís, ceramics; Ballarín & Andorrà, wrought iron; and Marcellí Gelabert, decorative painting.

42 Casa Evelí Planells

1924
Avinguda Diagonal 332 / Carrer de Sicília 195

Josep Maria Jujol, *architect*

While Casa Sayrach is usually considered the last *modernista* work, Casa Planells is even later. Although they include it in *Modernisme*, historians consider this building to be an anachronism. Like Gaudí, Jujol was a free spirit, which often makes it difficult to categorize him.

This is the project that solves the problem of its corner location in the most original way. At the same time, it marks the spectacular triumph of the curve and, thanks to a subtle interplay of blinds, endows voids with the quality of filled spaces: the whole facade is animated with relaxed movement. (It is a shame that the roofline was not completed according to Jujol's plan.) The interior is like a veritable living sculpture and features a number of highly original design details, such as the banisters of the staircase linking the two floors of the duplex. By virtue of the nakedness and austerity of the facade, and of the architect's desire to find a form, this work by Jujol may be considered an original contribution to expressionism.

(43) TEMPLE EXPIATORI DE LA SAGRADA FAMÍLIA
1882-1926
Carrer de Mallorca 403

ANTONI GAUDÍ I CORNET, *architect*

The Sagrada Família is Gaudí's most famous work, the one which is most closely identified with Barcelona in the popular imagination. Indeed it is possibly the most popular work in the whole of modern architecture.

Antoni Gaudí had nothing to do with the genesis of this ambitious project. The initiative came from the pious bookseller Josep Maria Bocabella, founder of the Associació Espiritual dels Devots de Sant Josep. It was in 1874 when the Mercedarian friar José María Rodríguez proposed the construction of a church by which to foster the association. The architect Francisco de Paula del Villar was engaged to draw up the plans, which he did in neo-Gothic style, and the project included a social center with schools, lounges, and other dependencies. However, technical disagreements with Joan Martorell, director of the works, led to the resignation of Paula del Villar, and it was then suggested that the young Gaudí take charge.

The personality and drive of the brilliant architect made their presence felt from the very outset, since not only did he entirely alter the aesthetics of the project, but he also endowed it with gigantic dimensions. And before drawing up detailed plans for the whole complex, he plunged into building the Nativity facade. Although his whole project was never completed, Gaudí left us with much that was achieved under his personal supervision.

The Gothic ground plan is in the form of a Latin cross, with five lengthwise naves, three of which are in the transept, with a deambulatory and an apse containing seven chapels and two staircases. An exterior cloister encircles the complex. The chapels were dedicated to the Virtues (Faith, Hope, and Charity), Baptism, Penitence and the couplets in honor of Saint Joseph.

While it is true that the vast dimensions of the Sagrada Família are immediately striking, the fact is that they are nothing compared to what Gaudí planned. For example, there was to have been a forest of no fewer than eighteen towers—one that would embody the Virgin, another representing Christ, one for each apostle and one for each evangelist. At 102 meters, the eight that were built seem to touch the sky, but are low in comparison to the planned central spire, which was to have risen up from the dome and be encrowned at a height of 178 meters by Gaudí's typical three-dimensional cross. It is difficult to imagine the total sensory impact such a project would have had on observers if completed. Gaudí had also planned for these towers a set of bells specially designed to be activated by the force of the wind; this explains the graded openings that reach up to the top of the spires.

Such an original ensemble had to be united by the strength of three facades, devoted to illustrating in a clear, didactic way the mysteries of the Nativity, the Passion, and the Resurrection. That period coincided with the emergence of the liturgical renovation movement, in which Gaudí was greatly interested by virtue of his considerable knowledge not only of the causes but also of the details of the change. We know that such interest was neither mere curiosity nor a speculative or abstract affinity, for the architect held long, intense conversations with bishops who not only had deep knowledge of the subject but had also formed personal opinions regarding the theme. It need not surprise us, therefore, that Gaudí should want to discover everything he could about the theme, given the task he had to carry out on the facades and his project for alterations to the Cathedral of Palma de Mallorca. And to express it visually he had recourse not only to

corporeal sculptures but also to less realistic, more esoteric elements, such as numbers and symbols.

The material Gaudí chose in order to give visual form to this religious world was stone, although the fact is that he had practically no other options if we bear in mind the sheer size of the project and the correspondingly enormous budget. There was no question, therefore, of using more expensive materials, such as bronze or wrought iron, characteristic of other cathedrals. Having therefore been forced to use stone, Gaudí had no doubts whatsoever about the crucial role light would play, above all when it came to modeling sculptures. Architecture is also the third dimension, and the architect considered that the strong, contrasting Mediterranean light was fundamental. He contended that no light upgraded and potentiated sculpture like the Mediterranean, both merging into an indissoluble unit.

Before Gaudí was run over and killed by a tram in 1926, he managed to complete the Nativity facade, a vast surface area devoted to telling the story of the life of the Infant Christ through the evocation of specific episodes. It is difficult to give a detailed description of the facade, since it is almost a baroque altarpiece informed by a highly generous sense of addition.

When we stand before the facade, we are faced by three great portals dedicated, from left to right, to Hope, Charity, and Faith. Above them, the three areas framed by large sculptures of the apostles. Following the same direction (left to right), we see Barnabas, Simon, Judas, Thaddeus, and Matthew. And just in front of these we glimpse the figures of angels heralding the Annunciation. The head of one of these is a portrait of the young artist Ricard Opisso.

Returning to the Portal of Hope, the following themes are represented sculpturally: the anagram of Saint Joseph; Jesus in the workshop at Nazareth; the betrothal of the Virgin and Saint Joseph; the flight into Egypt; the massacre of the innocents; the Roman soldier; the Infant and the flora of Palestine; the dead child; and the allegory of the mountain of Montserrat and of Saint Joseph.

On the central Portal of Charity: the birth; the manger; chaos and the mineral and vegetable worlds; the star of Bethlehem; the anagram of Jesus, the Eucharist; and the coronation of the Virgin. The gigantic crest features a fascinating colored ceramic cypress.

On the Portal of Faith: the anagram of Mary; the presentation of Jesus in the Temple; Jesus and the doctors of the Temple; Jesus the carpenter; the vegetation of Palestine; the immaculate conception; the lantern of faith; and the Holy Trinity.

A partial list of all the minor elements includes reptiles, snails, salamanders, hedgehogs, sea anemones, turtles and tortoises, lizards, seashells, cocks, hens, chicks, ducks, birds in flight, eagles, doves, seagulls, rooks, and nightingales. And as regards flora: cypresses, seaweeds, canes, mushrooms, roses, almond trees in flower, olives, oranges, ivy, moss, and so on.

Stone endows the whole ensemble with unity, although Gaudí had intended to introduce a considerable number of chromatic touches, such as the impressive green cypress spattered with white doves. Carlos Mani, Juan Matamala, and Busquets, who were far from the best in their field, contributed to the sculptural work, for which Gaudí experimented with making plaster casts of real models, human or animal, alive or dead, and also of objects. He also made photographs of models posed in a mirrored room, which enabled him to see a pose from all the angles simultaneously. While this in theory might seem interesting, even innovative, the fact is that the practical results fell far below expectations. And although some of Gaudí's closest collaborators attempted to draw his attention to the fact, it proved impossible to change his mind.

44 Hospital de la Santa Creu i de Sant Pau
1901–1930
Carrer de Sant Antoni Maria Claret / Carrer de Cartagena

Lluís Domènech i Montaner, *architect*

The two great hospitals that have marked the history of Barcelona reveal the extent to which power and civic responsibility may occasionally rise to circumstances. In 1401 King Martin the Humanist founded the Hospital de la Santa Creu, and such was his foresight that it was still operative at the beginning of this century. Late in the nineteenth century the banker Pau Gil donated 4 million pesetas for the construction of a hospital in keeping with the needs of the times, which gave rise to the foundation of the Hospital de la Santa Creu i de Sant Pau (this is its official name, although it is popularly known simply as the Hospital de Sant Pau, having gradually assimilated all the functions of its predecessor).

The dimensions that from the very outset this project acquired were truly spectacular. The sheer physical scale of the undertaking was eloquent enough even before work actually began: nine whole blocks in the *Eixample*. Furthermore, the choice of architect was evidence that the objective was excellence; indeed, Domènech i Montaner was then at the height of his career.

He presented his project in 1901.

A simple glance at his drawings of the complete complex reveals that Domènech clearly intended to create an alternative to Cerdà's *Eixample* plan. His refusal to obey the strict gridiron and his decision to orient his project diagonally confirmed, many decades later, his will to be on the front line, together with Puig i Cadafalch, in the battle against the dictates of the Cerdà plan.

Only the administrative pavilion (the main facade), two examination pavilions, six infirmary wards, and one operating theater had been completed when Gil's legacy ran out in 1911. However, the bourgeoisie of the time, aware of their civic responsibilities, provided the donations that made it possible for work to progress. Thus by 1928 the Sant Frederic, Sagrat Cor, and Sant Miquel dels Sants pavilions had been completed. The whole complex now totaled twenty-seven pavilions, although this was still far from the forty-eight Domènech had originally conceived.

In 1913 the hospital won the annual award granted by the city council for the best building of the year.

While Domènech's method had invariably been that of an orchestra conductor, whose baton directed a team of specialists and craftsmen, since his aim was to enhance his work with a veritable profusion of decorative arts, in the case of the hospital this method reached its zenith. This is understandable given the magnitude of the project, although many believed that such sumptuousness was unnecessary in a public health establishment. King Alfonso XIII, on the very day he officially inaugurated the hospital, commented, "You people of Barcelona are a true paradox: you build a palace for your sick and stables for your king." Domènech's "orchestra" included his son Pere, who assisted him from the outset, and who, on Domènech's death in 1923, built a number of pavilions that continued his father's style, although by 1928 he had introduced a note of eclecticism. Other collaborators were the architects Enric Català (technical and administrative aspects), Eusebi Bona (assistant), and Puig Janer (when required). Eusebi Arnau, one of Domènech's most faithful collaborators, also contributed, although most of the sculpture is by Pau Gargallo who, besides producing a prodigious number of pieces, also supervised the ornamental sculpture by Francesc Madurell. The painter Francesc Labarta was responsible for the other decorative arts, both painting, of course, and the design of the mosaics (executed by Mario Maragliano) and the ceramics, assisted by Lluís Gargallo, the sculptor's brother. The Barcelona firm of Pujol & Bausis and the Castellón firm of Elias Paris supplied the ceramic pieces. The wrought-iron work was by Josep Perpiñà. Cosme Toda, of Barcelona, and Mosaics Nolla, from Valencia, were responsible for the flooring. The marble was supplied by the firm of Josep Casals Comdor. Rigalt created the magnificent stained glass. Badia & Ferrer was responsible for the garden and Vilaró for the wall painting.

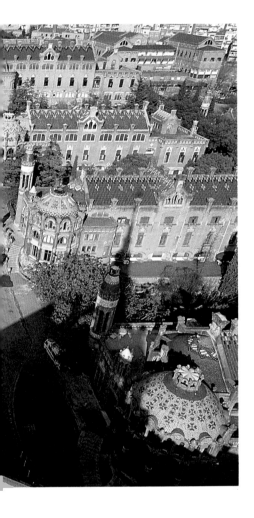

Domènech made a deep documentary study of the organization of large hospital complexes abroad and opted for the solution considered the most operative at the turn of the century: all the services and communication links between pavilions should be concentrated underground. Despite the dimensions of the complex, Domènech chose few materials, probably to obtain greater stylistic and visual unity. Brick is the main protagonist on the pavilion facades, and he also used flat brick for ceilings and roofs in accordance with an old Catalan tradition that *Modernisme* not only adopted but also enhanced. He also assigned a leading role to stone, from quarries in Girona, Vilaseca, and Barcelona. The use of marble, on the other hand, is very restrained, while touches of ceramics and mosaics provide decoration.

Seen from the exterior, the complex is characterized by great formal coherence, despite its large dimensions and the considerable number of pavilions widely scattered among trees and gardens. It is an exemplary work of urbanism, being more or less symmetrical on either side of a potent central axis. Seen from the interior, the complex is astonishingly grand, and on more than one occasion attains the solemnity appropriate to such a major institutional work.

The limits of the hospital grounds are marked by a solid stone wall, although at the main entrance, on the prominent corner of Sant Antoni Maria Claret and Cartagena, this wall becomes attractive wrought-iron railings featuring two columns, originally hollow to accommodate the porters' lodges and crowned by sculptures of Saint Paul and the holy cross, representing the official name of the institution. In the middle of the space separating the main gate from the great administrative pavilion, a magnificently delicate sculptural group by Eusebi Arnau pays homage to the generosity of Pau Gil.

This is the work in which Domènech i Montaner concentrated the greatest amount of symbology, since this project was the perfect opportunity to copiously apply floralism and heraldry, two fields in which the architect was a known authority and which he lovingly cultivated.

The administrative pavilion is by far the most important of the hospital buildings, given its function to receive visitors, represent the institution to the world, and constitute a visual screen for the complex. For this reason, it is the most attractive in terms of structure and ornamentation. Its exterior benefits from the epic air supplied by the high clock tower that dominates the center of the building, which opens as if winged. A substantial series of sculptures by Pau Gargallo combines with sixteen enormous panels, on which mosaics by Maragliano, based on designs by Labarta, recount with historic stringency the antecedents to hospital services and, needless to say, the steps leading to King Martin's founding of the Hospital de la Santa Creu, and eventually the founding of the Hospital de Sant Pau. The interior impresses the visitor with its vast space, which combines the porches at the vehicle entrance, the elegance of the main staircase, and the exceptional quality of a conference room in keeping with the solemnity required. Each of the two wings is closed at the end by a rectangular building; one contains the Library-Museum and the other the Secretariat-Archives. The left wing has suffered mutilations that affect not only the structure but also the ambience.

Decoration is everywhere, though stained glass does not enjoy the same prominence here as in other works; mosaic appears in the form of Labarta's designs and also acts as borders; ceramic tile covers large surfaces and was chosen because it is durable and easy to clean. However, the creative contribution that far outweighs the others is the set of sculptures entirely by Pau Gargallo, exceptional in terms both of quality and quantity.

The Hospital de la Santa Creu i de Sant Pau is a veritable *modernista* city within *modernista* Barcelona.

ⓐ⁵ Park Güell

1900–1914
Carrer d'Olot

Antoni Gaudí i Cornet, *architect*

Today we are in a position to appreciate this masterpiece of world art in all its creative grandeur, although the fact is that in its day it was considered an absolute failure. It was an avant-garde work, in the strict sense that it was ahead of its time: And not only in the artistic sense was it radically innovative. Gaudí's idea here was that of a garden city in which a number of communal services were to be provided, but the individualistic society of the time was not prepared to understand it. As if this were not enough, the site lay so far from the Barcelona of the time that people were very reluctant to embark upon an adventure that would disconnect them from the vital center of the city.

Güell asked Gaudí to draw up a project based on an idea that, according to some, was based on the English garden city and, according to others, on a complex he himself had seen in Nîmes, France. Whatever the case, it strikes me as significant that the entrance features the English word "Park."

The idea was to group together thirty-two extensive and previously delimited private plots that would enjoy a set of common facilities, such as a concierge, market, lighting, paved streets, and a public square.

The estate acquired by the patron for the purpose was on highly uneven ground. For this reason, Gaudí devoted the first two years to preparing the ground, though restricting himself to the essential minimum, since his aim was to merge architecture and nature. He therefore preserved as much as he could and traced out a set of paths that as far as possible followed the contours of the site. And when he had to build the inevitable viaducts, possibly the most aggressive elements, he used local stone to compose constructions evoking plant structures.

The precinct must be entered from Carrer d'Olot, since this marks the beginning of an initiatory route impossible to understand if one enters by any of the other gates. On the great wall surrounding the park appear the several medallions featuring the name "Park Güell" in *trencadís*, a fine example of the creation of a logotype. The main gate is flanked by two buildings, the one on the right originally the services pavilion and the one on the left, the porter's lodge, which reveal the architect's capacity to imagine suggestive forms that have no parallel in architecture. They remind us of fairy tales by the Brothers Grimm, above all if we contemplate the sculptural roof crowned by the hallucinogenic mushroom *Amanita Muscaria*. On top of a twelve-meter-high tower rises a needle a further seventeen meters high, which was destroyed in 1936, and a defective copy was put up. (The original work was discovered inside the porter's lodge in 1995, and it was put back in place in 1997.)

Opposite, the solemn, sinuous staircase begins; on either side, walls featuring ceramic pieces alternating between white and polychrome, both crowned by ceramic merlons. In the center, we gradually discover a medallion with the head of a serpent and the coat of arms of Catalonia, and then a gigantic lizard. It is said that once Gaudí had completed the wire-mesh frame of the animal's body, before covering it with trencadís he jumped up and down on it several times to make it arbitrarily and attractively warped. At the end, a polychrome border elegantly frames a central cavity, which became an improvised bench for visitors to take a rest. Gaudí was attracted by the caves he discovered on his excursions through Catalonia and also on this site, where he came across a cave (now closed) full of fossil remains of large prehistoric animals. He surely had such caves in mind when creating this bench and the similar one behind the main gate on the right.

This short rest prepares us to receive one of the greatest emotional and artistic impacts reserved for us. Indeed, although we glimpse it just above the shafts of a series of columns, it is impossible to anticipate the spectacle that awaits as we complete the climb up the stairs. This is the hypostyle chamber popularly known as the Chamber of the Hundred Columns, although in fact they number ninety-six. This space was planned to be the marketplace, and lies beneath and supports the great public square above. Inside each column there is a duct that carries filtered rainwater to a cistern. If both the visual impact and the atmosphere astound us, we are even more astonished when we lift our eyes and contemplate the disks that Jujol created with absolute freedom and with Gaudí's blessing. The unfettered imagination that characterized Jujol, as well as his cultivation of the gestural, led him to create a provocative avant-garde work. Indeed, he obtained his artistic results by combining the most unlikely elements, becoming thus a pioneer of collage and surrealism. The attentive observer will discover the head of a doll, plates, the ends of bottles, cups, glasses, and so on. Also worthy of note is the disk that, like the tentacles of an octopus, tries to enter space like a sculpture. In the intrados between certain domes Jujol executed compositions of notable plastic force.

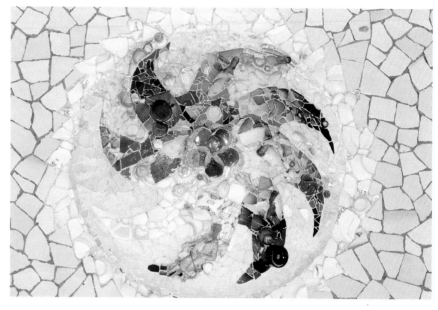

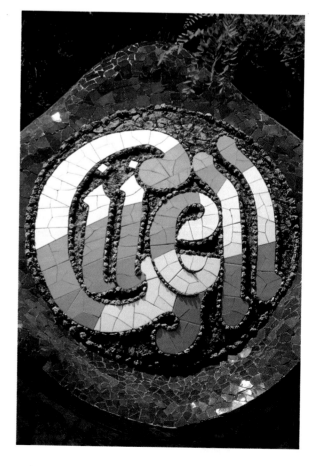

Above the hypostyle chamber is the great public square, a huge esplanade bordered by the most famous bench in the world. Gaudí obtained the profile of the bench by seating one of the workmen on it and taking his measurements. While its twists and turns are one of the unexpected attractions of the bench, equally successful was Gaudí's decision to give Jujol carte blanche to act according to the dictates of his vivid imagination. And the result is a thrilling, pioneering work of abstraction and collage. Once the workers had broken up the ceramics, often they were required to carefully recompose them in order not to break the original uniformity, not so much of color as of form. By virtue both of its enormous length and its quality, the bench continues to be a fascinating, audacious creation of great artistic force. Equal attention must be paid both to the front and the rear, although it can be hard to find the suitable angle and position from which to do so.

The fact that this urban adventure was such a resounding failure meant that only Martí Trias's show house, designed by Batllevell, and Gaudí's father's house, by Berenguer, were built. In 1910 Eusebi Güell entrusted Gaudí with alterations to the historical Casa Larrard in Can Muntaner, in which the Maecenas lived until his death. It was not until 1961 that Gaudí's family house was purchased by the private association Amics de Gaudí, which set up its headquarters there and converted it into a museum that was opened two years later, displaying souvenirs and works by a wide variety of entities.

The economic failure of the Park Güell venture led to Güell's heirs approaching the city to purchase it, convinced that no one else would want to do so. Despite public criticism of what the people felt was an unnecessary expenditure, the city council bought it in 1922, and the following year converted it into a municipal park open to the public.

In 1962 Park Güell was classified as an artistic monument, having been declared a national monument in 1909. In 1984 it was listed by UNESCO as part of the World Heritage Site.

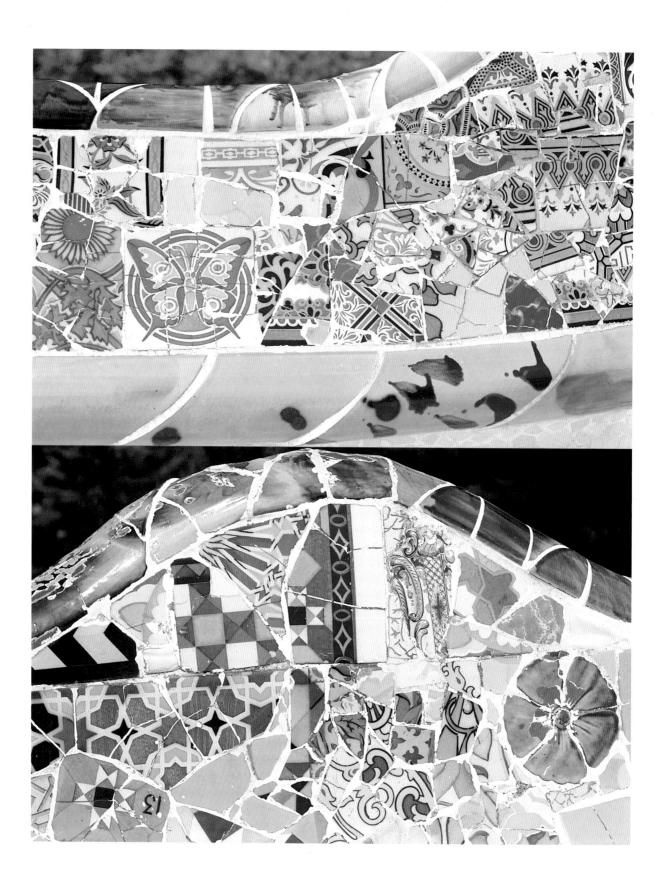

46 CASA MANUEL VICENS I MONTANER
1888
Carrer de les Carolines 24

ANTONI GAUDÍ I CORNET, *architect*

Casa Vicens was Gaudí's first major project. Manuel Vicens, owner of a ceramic and tile factory, commissioned the architect to build a single-family residence for him. The site was not particularly inspiring, bearing in mind the period: it belonged to the township of Gràcia and was rather modest (although less so than today, since the estate was originally almost twice as big and had a garden, which some decades ago was reduced in size so that the street could be widened). The most negative element, however, is the neighboring building, which does not exactly enhance the presence of the house.

The first thing Gaudí did was to visually reconnoiter the site, where he discovered two elements he decided to exploit: a palmetto leaf and a flower. From the leaf he created a module which, repeated ad infinitum, became the railings encircling the entire estate. When the garden was cut down in size, the part of this fine work that was removed was re-erected in the Park Güell. Using the yellow flower, a zinnia, as his model, he designed a tile, which Vicens himself manufactured, and used it as one of the elements that endows the house with its personality. In all, Gaudí chose three materials to compose the spectacular facades on three sides: brick, stone, and the stunning Valencia tiles (as a tribute to the client).

The exterior structure is highly original, governed by volume, angular volume with lines that enter into space, a concept far different from that of curved volume that informs La Pedrera. Elements jut out from the main body, many of them in the form of buttresses, while others are galleries or towers attached to the corners. The galleries and towers project farther at the top, which caused concern among the builders who feared that this would cause the building to collapse. Within a rigorously asymmetrical concept, the relationship between empty and full, between positive and negative, creates a fascinating, innovative interplay, revealing a self-confidence normally inconceivable in a young, inexperienced architect.

The historiated and openly *modernista* wrought-iron work is a subsequent intervention, and was not designed by Gaudí. On the other hand, the blinds are very interesting to Gaudí scholars. Though they are apparently Chinese in style, some experts, and also the architect Ignasi de Solà-Morales, consider them to be closer to the Mediterranean, and above all Arab, tradition. Whatever the case, the daring forms and bursts of color of Casa Vicens have a dazzling impact on the unsuspecting observer today. It is easy to imagine the astonishment that the house must have caused in its day, in a Gràcia characterized above all by gray monotony.

The interior is more conventional, fruit of an ornamental style that cultivates horror vacui. The finishes and intersections, which vary substantially depending on the kind of room or salon, endow the ensemble with a singular personality. I myself am enchanted by the tiny smokers' room, in which the descending sculptural ceiling reveals an unmistakably Arabic influence. All the decorative arts are present here in great diversity, though invariably governed by the unitarian concept imposed by Gaudí's energetic personality. Outstanding here is the work of the painter Josep Torrescassana and the sculptor Antoni Riba. The garden influence visible on the exterior also continues inside in the form of relief work on some ceilings, featuring vine leaves and arbutus.

Though it was Gaudí's first important work, Casa Vicens was awarded the prestigious prize granted annually by the Barcelona city council to the best new building of the year.

The current owners, the Herrero Jover family, honored to be able to live in a house by Gaudí but also aware of the responsibility this implies, decided in 1997 to restore not only the tiles and the exterior roofs but also to eliminate the coat of paint that the inconsiderate previous owner had applied to the sgraffiti that adorn some of the rooms.

ALTERNATIVE BUILDINGS ROUTE

1. PAVILION AND ENCLOSING WALL OF THE FINCA GÜELL
1887
Avinguda de Pedralbes 7

ANTONI GAUDÍ, *architect*

2. COLEGIO DE LAS TERESIANAS
1890
Carrer de Ganduxer 85–105

ANTONI GAUDÍ, *architect*

3. CASA BELLESGUARD
1902
Carrer de Bellesguard 16–20

ANTONI GAUDÍ, *architect*

4. FÁBRICA CASARRAMONA
1911
Carrer de Mèxic 36–44

JOSEP PUIG I CADAFALCH, *architect*

5. FINCA MIRALLES GATE
1902
Passeig Manuel Girona 75

ANTONI GAUDÍ, *architect*

6. FARMÀCIA PUIGORIOL
1914
Carrer de Mallorca 312

MARIANO PAU, *builder*

7. MONUMENT TO DOCTOR ROBERT
1910
Plaça de Tetuan

JOSEP LLIMONA, *sculptor*

8. Casa Roviralta (Frare Blanc)
1913
Avinguda del Tibidabo 31

Joan Rubió i Bellver, *architect*

9. Casa Macari Golferichs
1901
Gran Via de les Corts Catalanes 491

Joan Rubió i Bellver, *architect*

10. Casa Muley-Afid
1914
Passeig de la Bonanova 55

Josep Puig i Cadafalch, *architect*

11. Museu de Zoologia
1888
Parc de la Ciutadella

Lluís Domènech i Montaner, *architect*

12. Casa de Lactància
1913
Gran Via de les Corts Catalanes 475–477

Pere Falqués and
Antoni de Falguera, *architects*

13. Plaça de toros Monumental
1916
Gran Via de les Corts Catalanes, 749

Ignasi Mas and
Domènec Sugrañes, *architects*

14. Casa Provincial de Maternitat
1898
Travessera de les Corts 131–159

Camil Oliveras, *architect*

15. Central Catalana d'Electricitat
1899
Avinguda de Vilanova 12

Pere Falqués, *architect*